THE ULTIMATE WATER BATH CANNING FOR BEGINNERS

ENJOY 200+ FINEST GRANDMOTHER'S RECIPES HANDED DOWN FROM GENERATION TO GENERATION BY WORD OF MOUTH

Introduction

Since the invention of glass jars with ground glass joints, cooks have preserved food by hermetically sealing it in sterilized jars. Water bath canning was invented independently in other countries around the same time, such as France and Australia. This process has become known as canning. Water bath canning is a method of processing canned foods in which jars are filled with raw fruits or vegetables that have been precooked by blanching or boiling and then immersed in boiling water to cover for some time, such as 15 minutes.

Water bath canning is a technique that is used to preserve high acidic foods. This preservation method involves boiling water that is poured over the top of the food in a jar. Then, the pots are submerged into boiling water for an allotted time before they are removed and allowed to cool down. The food in the jar is sealed with a lid. The food is heated through the boiling water and then cooled through the cold water. This method is used to process foods that have high acidity to prevent harmful bacteria from growing.

Water bath canning has a dual purpose in the canning process. For one, it can preserve high acid foods such as tomatoes, peppers, and berries which would otherwise turn quickly if exposed to light or air for too long. Through the reduction of oxygen, the products can attain a long shelf life. Furthermore, water bath canning allows the food to reach a final storage temperature of 140 degrees Fahrenheit (60 degrees Celsius) to ensure that all microbes are killed. The jars are then cooled in their current state before they are sealed and put into storage. Foods should have a pH of 4 or lower to be preserved through water bath canning. The acidity of food is generally maintained by adding vinegar, wine or other acidic ingredients. Vegetables in water bath canning are typically prepared by blanching them in boiling water for a brief period. The vegetables are then removed from the boiling water and placed into jars that have been previously sterilized with boiling water or hot vinegar. Water bath canning is an ideal method of preserving for many reasons. Still, the most important is that it allows for the integrity of your food to be maintained and your food to retain its natural taste. The only way water bath canning destroys much of the natural flavors and nutrients that are contained in your food is by reducing a simple sugar or acid such as vinegar.

Water bath canning is a safe and easy way to begin preserving your food simply and effectively. This book will focus on water bath canning fruits, vegetables, jam and jellies, and much more. There are various advantages that you will have when you begin preserving your foods—in addition to saving money. You will be able to prolong the growing season since you can use products that would not be ripe or mature at certain times of the year. You will also customize the recipes to make your food taste exactly how you want it.

Chapter 1.   The Benefits of Water Bath Canning

The main reason why you should start water bath canning is the health benefits. Preserving foods can make them last a lot longer, but it can also help you protect the vitamins and nutrients that are often diminished with other preservation methods. Water bath canning is a best way to preserve those foods you love to eat all year round, and it's easy to do when you have the right equipment.

You'll preserve the most nutrients when using a water bath canner to put up your vegetables and home-canned fruit. The canning process makes the food last much longer. Many people prefer using this method because it doesn't add chemicals as other forms do, so the food doesn't lose its flavor over time.

Here are the benefits:

- You'll keep the vitamins and nutrients in your food:
- You'll get a lot of satisfaction from knowing that you put up your food.
- Food tastes better when you use this method to preserve it.
- Water Bath Canners are easy to use, making them safer for you and the people in your home.
- The food lasts a lot longer. There won't be any mold or bacteria growing in the containers because they aren't sealed (you'll do this after the canning process).
- The food is more enjoyable and tastes better.
- You won't have to worry about bacteria, mold, or anything like that.
- Your food will stay safe for a much longer time.
- You can preserve your summer produce so that you can enjoy it in the wintertime.

Water bath canning is one of the best ways to preserve food, but it can be a little bit tricky at first. It's essential to keep things clean and organized throughout the entire process so that you don't end up putting your family in danger.

1. Water Bath Canning Advantages

You will be able to adore all the healthy food that comes out of your garden and have them last for a lot longer time than if you try other preserves. Distribution is also easy with this method; you'll be able to share your home-canned food with everyone around you or keep it for your own family. You'll have a more enjoyable time when you water bath canning because fresh fruits are more delicious when adequately preserved and canned.

1. You can preserve foods in jars that have a preservation time of 8 to 12 months, depending on the thickness of your food.
2. Water bath canning preserves foods at their peak condition in taste, texture and nutrition.
3. It is a fast, easy and safe technique to do the water bath canning process without having any special techniques or equipment
4. Water bath canning preserves food in the freshest and best quality for several years.
5. It is economical as a method of food preservation, as processing is done at a fraction of the cost of freezing or refrigeration
6. Water bath canning does not require special tools, so there is no additional cost for that.
7. You can preserve a variety of foods and keep them in your pantry without having to keep track of various jars filled with different types of preserves.
8. Water bath canning is an easy and inexpensive way to preserve various foods to enjoy for many years.
9. Water bath canning preserves food in the best possible quality as it makes sure that food remains safe, tasty and nutritious.
10. There's no need to be worried about time and temperature while doing water bath canning as it has been proved in many studies to be the safest method amongst all other preservation methods

With water bath canning, it is straightforward to preserve your garden veggies and even fruits. It is one of the best ways of keeping food to have something to eat even when there is a lack of fresh vegetables or fruits. With water bath canning, you will be able to preserve many things for different types of dishes, such as salsa, pickles, jams and more.

Chapter 2.   What do you need for your water bath canning?

Water bath canning is the easiest way to preserve your favorite foods, and it doesn't require any expensive equipment. All you need for this method are jars, lids and rings, a large pot, a stovetop or camping stove with an ovenproof dish that fits inside the pot, water, salt (optional), food to be canned. Water is the key ingredient, so make sure it's clean. It should be as free from impurities as possible so that bacteria don't grow in it. It doesn't need distilled water, but you may want to use filtered or bottled water if your tap water isn't outstanding quality. A charcoal filter can help remove any chlorine in the water.

It's important to always use new jars and lids for home canning and follow proper procedures to ensure food safety. If there are any fracture or chips in your jars, or if the lids aren't sealed correctly after processing, they could harbor bacteria, leading to food spoilage.

For this canning method, you will need half pint, pint, and ½-pint (8 ounces) jars. The size isn't essential as long as they're the same size. You'll only need enough jars to hold the amount of food you're preserving for a small canning session. For a larger batch, you'll need more jars. To can foods in jars, you'll need to sterilize the jars, lids, and rings.

1. How to prepare the jars for water bath canning:

To sterilize the jars, wash them in hot soapy water. Wash them properly and leave them to dry thoroughly on a towel.

When you are ready to begin canning your food, fill a large pot with water and bring it to a boil. Heat the water until it reaches a steady rolling boil (around 180-190 degrees). Pour the canning jars and lids into the boiling water, one at a time, so that they are entirely submerged. Leave them there for 10 minutes. This is imperative in ensuring that your jars are sterile - you'll know it's done when you see steam coming off the jars. If the water isn't boiling, put it on high heat until it is. When the jars and lids have been sterilized, drain them thoroughly, leaving only ¼- to ½ inch of water in the pot. Ladle the water bath into your jars. Take the jars upside down on a towel and let them cool completely, usually about 30 minutes.

To set your jars for water bath canning, follow these steps:
1. Wash your jars and contents thoroughly with hot soapy water.
2. Fill hot jars with hot food; never fill with cold food.
3. Remove air bubbles by sliding a spatula around the inside of the jar. Make sure that the contents are not touching the sides of the jar, as this may cause your jars to break when they are sterilized.
4. Wipe off any food spillover on rims and threads (where the lid will be screwed on).
5. Set the lids out of the hot water and screw them on tightly.
6. Place jars in a steamer or large pot of boiling water.
7. Boil for at least 20 minutes for high-acid canned food (20 minutes is needed to ensure that all high-acid food is heated to a temperature above the boiling point of 212 F/100 C, which will destroy any harmful bacteria).
8. Fill the pot with cold water, bring it back to a boil, lower the heat, and let it parboil for an hour or two.
9. Take off the pot from the heat, and leaving them upside down, leave it for a few hours. Please do not remove the jars from their water bath until completely cooled at room temperature, usually about 30 to 60 minutes.

2. How to seal the jars

Pour boiling water over the lids and then allow them to cool. Make sure that they are completely cool before screwing on the rings and putting on the lids.

When you are finished with the water bath, remove the jars from the pot and set them upside down so that the lid is facing up. Label each jar. Store them in a dark place for up to 1 year in temperatures between 65-80 degrees F (18-27 degrees C) under normal conditions. Store them for up to 3 years if you keep them in the refrigerator. If stored in temperatures above 80 degrees F (27 degrees C), they can be stored for only one year. Before opening a jar, make sure it is completely sealed with no jar left unsealed so that none of your food is exposed to air. If your jar remains unsealed after 6 months, don't consume the food in that jar.

Once you reach the end of your food, reseal it in an air-tight container and place it into the fridge or freezer for future use.

3. Tips for success with Water Bath Canning:

1. Be sure you sterilize your jars, lids, and rings appropriately by following the proper water bath canning procedures.
2. When you are ready to begin canning your food, make sure that your jars are completely submerged in boiling water before adding the lids and rings. This is important to ensure that any bacteria in the air are killed by the boiling water during processing.
3. Make sure that your jars are well sealed before putting them into their water bath. It's best to leave them upside down after the water bath to ensure that they are appropriately sealed.
4. Always use new lids and rings when you are canning to ensure food safety.
5. If you're canning larger quantities of food (more than 8 quarts), make sure that you have enough jars for food you're preserving for.
6. It's essential to use new lids and rings when you begin canning.
7. Check your temperatures throughout the entire water bath process so that you know for sure that the temperature of your jars is high enough. The ideal temperature for most food preservation is 200 F/93 C, although low-acid foods can be preserved at temperatures as low as 140°F/60 C.
8. Make sure that your jars are well sealed before putting them into their water bath.

In this process, you will be canning your food in jars using a regular water bath. You will be placing tightly sealed jars into a large pot of boiling water for several minutes. You will then fill the jars with your prepared food and cover them with the lids.

If you are preserving high-acid foods, remember to bring your hot-filled jars to a boil before putting on the lids and sealing them.

Chapter 3.   Jam and Jellies

1.   Caramel Apple Butter

Preparation time: 15 minutes   **Cooking time:** 35 minutes to 1 hour 20 minutes   **Servings:** 4 half-pints jar

Ingredients:

- 2½ pounds apples (about 8 large), cored and chopped (do not peel)
- ½ cup water
- ½ cup brandy
- 1 tablespoon bottled lemon juice
- 1 teaspoon pure vanilla extract
- 2¼ cups sugar

Directions:

1. In a pot or Dutch oven over low heat, combine the apples and water and cook until soft, about 20 minutes. Let cool for 30 minutes.
2. Set the apples in a blender or food processor or use an immersion blender. Measure the puree—you should have about 4½ cups.
3. Return the puree to the saucepan. Add the brandy, lemon juice, vanilla, and sugar. Cook until the mixture is fuzzy enough to mound on a spoon.
4. Ladle into 4 clean half-pints jar, leaving ¼-inch headspace. Top with two-piece lids and rings and close until finger-tight. Set in a water bath canner for 10 minutes, plus your altitude adjustment.

Nutrition:

Calories: 96   Carbs: 0g

Fat: 1.7g   Protein: 20.08g

2. Blueberry Cherry Butter

Preparation time: 30 minutes   **Cooking time:** 35 minutes to 1 hour 20 minutes   **Servings:** 6 half-pints jar

Ingredients:

- 3 pounds fresh sweet cherries, pitted and chopped
- 1½ pounds fresh blueberries
- 3 cups granulated sugar

Directions:

1. In a pot or Dutch oven over low heat, combine the cherries and blueberries and cook until soft, attaching small amounts of water if necessary to prevent scorching, about 20 minutes. Let cool for at least 30 minutes.
2. Set the fruit in a blender or food processor or use an immersion blender. Measure the puree—you should have about 6 cups.
3. Return the puree to the saucepan. Add the sugar. Cook until the mixture is fuzzy enough to mound on a spoon. This could take as little as 15 minutes or as long as an hour, depending on the size of your saucepan and the humidity in your kitchen.
4. Ladle into 6 clean half-pints jar, leaving ¼-inch headspace. Top with two-piece lids and rings and close until finger-tight. Set in a water bath canner for 10 minutes, plus your altitude adjustment.

Nutrition:

Calories: 244.2   Carbs: 11.2g

Fat: 8.3g   Protein: 31.3g

3. Golden Fruit Butter

Preparation time: 15 minutes, plus 30 minutes cooking time   **Cooking time:** 35 minutes to 1 hour 20 minutes   **Servings:** 4 half-pints jar or 8 quarter-pints jar

Ingredients:

- 1 large mango (about 1 pound), peeled, pitted, and chopped
- 3 medium peaches (about 1 pound), peeled, pitted, and chopped
- 3 medium yellow plums (about 8 ounces), pitted and quartered
- 12 apricots (about 1½ pounds), pitted and quartered
- 2 tablespoons bottled lime juice
- 2 cups granulated sugar

Directions:

1. In a pot or Dutch oven over low heat, combine the mango, peaches, plums, and apricots and cook until soft, 20 to 30 minutes, adding small amounts of water if necessary to prevent scorching. Let cool for at least 30 minutes.
2. Set the fruit in a blender or food processor or use an immersion blender. Measure the puree—you should have about 4 cups.
3. Return the puree to the saucepan. Add the lime juice and sugar. Cook until the mixture has thickened.
4. Ladle into 4 clean half-pints jar or 8 quarter-pints jar, leaving ¼-inch headspace. Top with two-piece lids and rings and close until finger-tight. Set in a water bath canner for 10 minutes, plus your altitude adjustment.

Nutrition:

Calories: 250

Fat: 19g

Carbs: 0g

Protein: 19g

4. Pear and Pineapple Jam

Preparation time: 15 minutes   **Cooking time:** 30 minutes   **Servings:** 6 pints jar

Ingredients:

- 2 pounds pears, peeled, pitted, and chopped
- 1 pound pineapple, peeled, cored and chopped
- 1 tablespoon lemon juice
- 1 cup sugar
- Zest from 1 lemon

Directions:

1. Sterilize the bottles in a water bath canner. Allow the bottles to cool.
2. Set all ingredients in a saucepan and bring to a boil over medium flame.
3. Set the heat to medium low and allow simmering for 15 minutes while stirring constantly.
4. Turn off the heat and allow cooling slightly.
5. Transfer the mixture to sterilized bottles and remove the air bubbles. Close the lid.
6. Bring in a water bath canner and process for 10 minutes.
7. Consume within a year.

Nutrition:

Calories: 174

Protein: 1.1 g

Carbs: 44.8 g

Fat: 0.4

Sugar: 37.9g

5. Guava Jam

Preparation time: 15 minutes   **Cooking time:** 1 hour 25 minutes   **Servings:** 8 pints jar

Ingredients:

- 6 ripe guavas (overripe preferred)
- 3 cups water
- Juice from 3 limes, freshly squeezed
- 1 cup sugar
- 2 tablespoons pectin

Directions:

1. Sterilize the bottles in a water bath canner. Allow the bottles to cool.
2. Chop the guavas and place in a saucepan. Spill in water and bring to a boil for 60 minutes,
3. Turn off the heat and strain the juice. Discard the solids.
4. On a clean pot, place the juice and stir in the lime juice and sugar. Set on the heat and bring to a boil over medium flame. Reduce the heat to simmer for another 10 minutes. Add in the pectin stir for 2 more minutes.
5. Turn off the heat and allow cooling slightly.
6. Transfer the mixture to sterilized bottles and remove the air bubbles. Close the lid.
7. Bring in a water bath canner and process for 10 minutes.
8. Consume within a year.

Nutrition:

Calories: 68

Protein: 0.1g

Carbs: 14g

Fat: 0.1g

Sugar: 10g

6. Blackberry Jam

Preparation time: 15 minutes   **Cooking time:** 30 minutes   **Servings:** 10 pints jar

Ingredients:

- 5 cups blackberries
- 2 cups sugar
- 2 tablespoons lemon juice

Directions:

1. Sterilize the bottles in a water bath canner. Allow the bottles to cool.
2. Place all ingredients in a saucepan. Set to a boil while stirring constantly for 10 minutes. Reduce the heat to simmer until the sauce thickens.
3. Set off the heat and allow to cool slightly.
4. Transfer the mixture to sterilized bottles and remove the air bubbles. Close the lid.
5. Set in a water bath canner and process for 10 minutes.
6. Consume within a year.

Nutrition:

Calories: 196

Protein: 1.7g

Carbs: 49.7g

Fat: 0.2g

Sugar: 44.9g

7. Blackcurrant Jam

Preparation time: 15 minutes

Cooking time: 30 minutes   **Servings:** 6 pints jar

Ingredients:

- 3 pounds blackcurrants
- 2 ½ pounds sugar
- 3 tablespoons lemon juice, freshly squeezed

Directions:

1. Sterilize the bottles in a water bath canner. Allow the bottles to cool.
2. Place all ingredients in a saucepan. Bring to a boil over medium heat. Swirl constantly to avoid the mixture from burning. Set the heat to low and parboil for another 10 minutes until the mixture thickens.
3. Set off the heat and allow the mixture to slightly cool.
4. Transfer the mixture to sterilized bottles and remove the air bubbles. Close the lid.
5. Set in a water bath canner and process for 10 minutes.
6. Consume within a year.

Nutrition:

Calories: 587   Fat: 0.6g

Protein: 2.1g   Sugar: 135g

Carbs: 149g

8. Kumquat Jam

Preparation time: 15 minutes   **Cooking time:** 30 minutes   **Servings:** 4 half pints jar

Ingredients:

- 2 cups kumquats, peeled and seeded   • 1 cup sugar
- 3 cups water

Directions:

1. Sterilize the bottles in a water bath canner. Allow the bottles to cool.
2. Set all ingredients in a saucepan and bring to a boil over medium flame. Reduce the heat to low and parboil for another 15 minutes or until the mixture thickens.
3. Set off the heat and allow the mixture to slightly cool.
4. Transfer the mixture to sterilized bottles and remove the air bubbles. Close the lid.
5. Bring in a water bath canner and process for 10 minutes.
6. Consume within a year.

Nutrition:

Calories: 89   Fat: 0.5g

Protein: 1.1 g   Sugar: 17.5g

Carbs: 21.5g

9. Honeyberry Jam

Preparation time: 15 minutes   **Cooking time:** 25 minutes   **Servings:** 4 half pints jar

Ingredients:

- 2 cups honeyberry fruit   • 2 cups sugar

Directions:

1. Sterilize the bottles in a water bath canner. Allow the bottles to cool.
2. Place all ingredients in a saucepan. Macerate the berries using a potato masher or a ladle.
3. Turn on the heat to medium high and bring to a boil while stirring constantly. Reduce the heat the medium low and allow to simmer for another 15 minutes or until the mixture thickens.
4. Set off the heat and allow the mixture to slightly cool.
5. Transfer the mixture to sterilized bottles and remove the air bubbles. Close the lid.
6. Bring in a water bath canner and process for 10 minutes.
7. Consume within a year.

Nutrition:

Calories: 190   Fat: 0.01g

Protein: 0.3g   Sugar: 47.4g

Carbs: 48.9g

10. Blueberry Vanilla Jam

Preparation time: 15 minutes   **Cooking time:** 22 minutes   **Servings:** 6 half pints jar

Ingredients:

- 6 large canning bottles
- 1 ¼ pounds blueberries, rinsed and stems removed
- ¾ cup granulated sugar
- 2 tablespoons lemon juice
- ½ vanilla bean pod, seeds scraped
- 1 teaspoon pectin

Directions:

1. Sterilize the bottles in a water bath canner. Allow the bottles to cool.
2. Place all ingredients except for the pectin in a pot and mash until the blueberries are macerated.
3. Set on the heat and bring to a boil for 10 minutes while stirring constantly. Remove the vanilla bean pod and stir in the pectin. Continue stirring for another 2 minutes until the mixture becomes thick.
4. Ladle into the sterilized jars and leave ¼ inch of headspace. Remove the air bubbles and screw the lid on.
5. Place in a water bath canner and follow the general instructions for water bath canning.
6. Process for 10 minutes.
7. Consume within a year and keep refrigerated once the bottles are opened.

Nutrition:

Calories: 38   Fat: 0.2g

Protein: 0.19g   Sugar: 8.7g

Carbs: 9.2g

11. Mandarin Orange Jam

Preparation time: 15 minutes   **Cooking time:** 22 minutes   **Servings:** 5 pints jar

Ingredients:

- 5 bottling jars with lid
- 2 pounds mandarin oranges, peeled and seeded (about 10 to 12 oranges)
- Juice from 1 lemon, freshly squeezed
- 1 cup sugar

Directions:

1. Sterilize the bottles in a water bath canner.

2. Chop the mandarin oranges roughly. Place the ingredients except the pectin in a pot and heat over medium flame. Stir constantly for 10 minutes to avoid burning at the bottom.
3. Stir in pectin and stir for another 2 minutes.
4. Set off the heat and allow to cool.
5. Transfer the orange jam into the sterilized bottles and make sure that there is ¼ headspace left. Remove the air bubbles. Close the lid.
6. Place the bottles in the water bath canner. Process for 10 minutes.
7. Consume within a year.

Nutrition:

Calories: 169

Protein: 1.3g

Carbs: 41.6g

Fat: 0.2g

Sugar: 35g

12. Maple Blackberry Jam

Preparation time: 15 minutes   **Cooking time:** 60 minutes   **Servings:** 6 pints jar

Ingredients:

- 6 canning bottles
- 6 cups blackberries, crushed
- 1 ½ cup pure maple syrup
- Zest and juice from one lemon

Directions:

1. Sterilize the bottles in a water bath canner. Allow the bottles to cool.
2. Set all ingredients in a saucepan and bring to a simmer. Cook for 50 minutes while stirring constantly over medium low heat or until the mixture thickens.
3. Dip an old spoon into the jam and tip gently. If it runs off in a sheet and if the liquid does not drip, the jam is ready.
4. Set off the heat and allow the mixture to slightly cool before transferring into the sterilized bottles.
5. Remove the air bubbles in the mixture. Close the lid and place in the water bath canner.
6. Process for 10 minutes.
7. Store in a cool dark place and consume within a year.

Nutrition:

Calories: 379

Protein: 2.9g

Carbs: 96g

Fat: 0.4g

Sugar: 84.2g

13. Pineapple Jam

Preparation time: 15 minutes   **Cooking time:** 1 hour 10 minutes   **Servings:** 2 pints jar

Ingredients:

- 2 canning bottles
- 1 cup sugar
- 2 fresh lemons, juiced
- 1 medium-sized pineapple, peeled and chopped

Directions:

1. Sterilize the bottles in a water bath canner. Allow the bottles to cool.
2. Add all ingredients in a medium-sized pot and bring to a boil. Reduce the heat and simmer to an hour until the liquid has evaporated and the mixture thickens.
3. Set off the heat and allow to slightly cool before transferring into the bottles.
4. Remove the air bubbles and close the lid.
5. Set in a water bath canner and process for 10 minutes.
6. Consume within a year.

Nutrition:

Calories: 216
Protein: 1.3g
Carbs: 56.3g

Fat: 0.3g
Sugar: 47.3g

14. Cherry Jam

Preparation time: 15 minutes   **Cooking time:** 60 minutes   **Servings:** 4 pints jar

Ingredients:

- 4 canning bottles
- 2 pounds cherries, stems removed and pitted
- 2 ½ cups sugar
- Juice from 1 lemon, freshly squeezed
- 2 drops of almond extract

Directions:

1. Sterilize the bottles in a water bath canner. Allow the bottles to cool.
2. Place all ingredients in a saucepan and cook for 40 minutes or until the mixture thickens. Continue swirling to prevent the bottom from burning.
3. Turn off the heat and remove from the pot to slightly cool.
4. Transfer to the bottles. Remove the air bubbles and close the lid.
5. Set in a water bath canner and process for 10 minutes.
6. Consume within a year.

Nutrition:

Calories: 331
Protein: 1.9g
Carbs: 83.6g

Fat: 0.6g
Sugar: 78.7g

15. Raspberry Jam

Preparation time: 15 minutes   **Cooking time:** 27 minutes   **Servings:** 4 pints jar

Ingredients:

- 4 canning bottles with lid
- 4 cups crushed ripe raspberries
- 1 tablespoon fresh lemon juice
- 6 ½ cups sugar
- ½ teaspoon unsalted butter
- 3-ounce pectin

Directions:

1. Sterilize the bottles in a water bath canner. Allow the bottles to cool.
2. Macerate the raspberries and run through a colander to remove the seeds.
3. Place the strained raspberries in a pot and stir in the lemon juice, sugar, and butter.
4. Set on the heat to medium and bring to a rolling boil for 10 minutes. Reduce the heat to simmer for 5 minutes before adding the pectin. Allow to simmer for another 2 minutes.
5. Turn off the heat to cool.
6. Transfer the jam to sterilized bottles and remove the air bubbles.
7. Close the lid.
8. Bring in a water bath canner and process for 10 minutes.
9. Consume within a year.

Nutrition:

Calories: 581
Protein: 1.4g
Carbs: 148g

Fat: 0.4g
Sugar: 5.9g

16. Plum Butter

Preparation time: 15 minutes   **Cooking time:** 25 minutes   **Servings:** 6 pints jar

Ingredients:

- 6 canning bottles
- 6 pounds Italian plums, halved and pits removed
- 4 cups sugar
- 1 ½ teaspoons ground cinnamon
- ½ teaspoons ground cloves

Directions:
1. Sterilize the bottles in a water bath canner. Allow the bottles to cool.
2. Place the plums, sugar, cinnamon, and cloves in a saucepan.
3. Set on the heat and bring to a rolling boil for 10 minutes. Reduce the heat to low and continue stirring until the mixture becomes thick.
4. Turn off the heat to cool.
5. Transfer the jam to sterilized bottles and remove the air bubbles. Close the lid.
6. Set in a water bath canner and process for 10 minutes.
7. Consume within a year.

Nutrition:
Calories: 332

Protein: 3.8g

Carbs: 86.2g

Fat: 0.2g

Sugar: 83.2g

17. Apple Pie Jam

Preparation time: 15 minutes   **Cooking time:** 27 minutes   **Servings:** 6 pints jar

Ingredients:

- 6 canning bottles
- 4 cups diced apples
- 2 tablespoons lemon juice, freshly squeezed
- 1 ¼ teaspoon ground cinnamon
- ¼ teaspoon ground ginger
- ¼ teaspoon ground nutmeg
- 4 cups granulated sugar
- 1 cup packed brown sugar
- ½ teaspoon unsalted butter
- 1 box pectin

Directions:
1. Sterilize the bottles in a water bath canner. Allow the bottles to cool.
2. Place the apples, lemon juice, cinnamon, ginger, nutmeg, sugar, and butter in a saucepan.
3. Turn on the heat and allow simmering for 15 minutes. Stir in the pectin and simmer for 2 minutes. Keep swirling to avoid the mixture from burning.
4. Turn off the heat to cool.
5. Transfer the mixture to sterilized bottles and remove the air bubbles. Close the lid.
6. Set in a water bath canner and process for 10 minutes.
7. Consume within a year.

Nutrition:
Calories: 275

Protein: 0.2g

Carbs: 70.6g

Fat: 0.3g

Sugar: 66.9g

18. Star Fruit Jam

Preparation time: 15 minutes   **Cooking time:** 30 minutes   **Servings:** 2 pints jar

Ingredients:

- 2 canning bottles
- 1 ¼ pounds carambolas or star fruit, edges trimmed and chopped
- 1 cup water
- 2 cups white sugar
- Juice from 1 lemon, freshly squeezed

Directions:
1. Sterilize the bottles in a water bath canner. Allow the bottles to cool.

2. Place all ingredients in a saucepan. Set on the heat and bring the mixture to a simmer. Stir for 20 minutes or until the mixture is thick and the liquid has reduced.
3. Set off the heat and allow the mixture to cool down.
4. Transfer the mixture to sterilized bottles and remove the air bubbles. Close the lid.
5. Bring in a water bath canner and process for 10 minutes.
6. Consume within a year.

Nutrition:

Calories: 241

Protein: 1.5g

Carbs: 60.3g

Fat: 0.5g

Sugar: 54.6g

19. Nectarine Brown Sugar Jam

Preparation time: 15 minutes   **Cooking time:** 25 minutes   **Servings:** 8 pints jar

Ingredients:

- 6 to 8 canning bottles
- 4 pounds nectarines, peeled, seeded and chopped
- 1 ½ cup brown sugar, lightly packed
- 4 tablespoons lemon juice
- ½ teaspoon cinnamon
- ¼ teaspoon ground ginger

Directions:

1. Sterilize the bottles in a water bath canner. Allow the bottles to cool.
2. Place all ingredients in a big saucepan and bring to a rolling boil for 5 minutes. Set the heat to low and parboil for another 10 minutes. Keep stirring until the mixture thickens.
3. Set off the heat and allow to cool slightly.
4. Transfer the mixture to sterilized bottles and remove the air bubbles. Close the lid.
5. Bring in a water bath canner and process for 10 minutes.
6. Consume within a year.

Nutrition:

Calories: 259

Protein: 2.5g

Carbs: 65.2g

Fat: 0.8g

Sugar: 58.1g

20. Strawberry Jam

Preparation time: 15 minutes   **Cooking time:** 1 hour and 20 minutes   **Servings:** 2 pints jar

Ingredients:

- 2 pints jar
- 2 pounds ripe strawberries, hulled and cleaned
- 2 ½ cups sugar
- 1 tablespoon freshly squeezed orange juice

Directions:

1. Sterilize the bottles in a water bath canner. Allow the bottles to cool.
2. Chop the strawberries and place all ingredients in a large pan. Let it sit for an hour until the sugar is dissolves and the mixture become watery.
3. Heat over the stove using medium flame and bring to a boil. Make sure to stir constantly and mashing with the ladle to macerate. Cook for 10 minutes then allow to cool.
4. Place the strawberry jam in sterilized bottles.
5. Set in a water bath canner and process for 10 minutes.
6. Consumer within a year.

Nutrition:

Calories: 318

Protein: 1.6g

Carbs: 80.2g   Sugar: 73g

Fat: 0.7g

21. Fig Jam

Preparation time: 15 minutes   **Cooking time:** 25 minutes   **Servings:** 1 pint jar

Ingredients:

- 1-pint jar
- 1-pound black figs
- ¾ cup granulated sugar
- ¼ cup water
- Juice from ½ small lemon, freshly squeezed
- 1 teaspoon pure vanilla extract

Directions:

1. Sterilize the bottle in a water bath canner. Allow the bottles to cool.
2. Place the figs in a blender and puree until smooth. Place the pureed figs in a pot and add in the rest of the ingredients.
3. Bring to a boil over medium flame while stirring constantly. Cook for 10 minutes and remove from the heat.
4. Allow to cool before transferring into the sterilized bottle.
5. Follow the general instructions for water bath canning and can for 15 minutes.
6. Consume within a year.

Nutrition:

Calories: 357   Fat: 1.1g

Protein: 3.8g   Sugar: 72.8g

Carbs: 92g

22. Jalapeño Pepper Jelly

Preparation time: 90 minutes   **Cooking time:** 20 minutes   **Servings:** 5 half pints jar

Ingredients:

- 1 Cup, chopped green bell pepper
- ⅓ Cup of chopped jalapeño pepper
- 4 Cups of sugar
- 1 Cup of cider vinegar
- 1 Packet of pectin, about 6 ounces

Directions:

1. Merge all the ingredients together in a large saucepot, and let it boil for about five minutes.
2. Next, let it cool to room temperature for about one hour, and then put them into jars.
3. Set the jars sit in a water bath for five minutes, and then let them sit at room temperature for about twelve to 24 hours before storing.

Nutrition:

Calories: 651   Protein: 17g

Fat: 26g   Sodium: 112mg

Carbs: 93g

23. Cranberry Orange Jelly

Preparation time: 10 minutes   **Cooking time:** 5 minutes   **Servings:** 6 half-pints jar

Ingredients:

- 3½ cups unsweetened cranberry juice
- 1 (1.75-ounce) box Sure-Jell or other powdered pectin
- 5 cups granulated sugar
- Grated zest of 1 large orange

Directions:

1. In a pot or Dutch oven over high heat, combine the cranberry juice and pectin. Bring to a boil, stirring to combine.
2. Add the sugar, stirring until it dissolves. Add the orange zest. Set the mixture to a full boil and boil for 1 minute, stirring constantly. Detach from the heat and skim off the foam.
3. Ladle into 6 clean half-pints jar, leaving ¼-inch headspace. Top with two-piece lids and rings and close until finger-tight. Set in a water bath canner for 10 minutes.

Nutrition:

Calories: 202

Fat: 2.3 g

Carbs: 31.4 g

Fiber: 12.6 g

Protein: 14.8

24. Apple Kiwi Calvados Jelly

Preparation time: 20 minutes, plus 6 hours straining time

Cooking time: 40 to 55 minutes

Servings: 2 half-pints jar

Ingredients:

- 2½ pounds apples (about 6 large), cut into wedges (do not peel or core)
- 1 pound kiwi (about 6), cut into wedges (do not peel)
- ¼ cup apple brandy
- 3 cups water
- 2 cups granulated sugar

Directions:

1. In a pot or Dutch oven, combine the apples, kiwi, brandy, and water. Cover and bring to a boil over high heat. Set the heat and simmer until the fruit is soft, about 20 minutes. Let cool slightly.
2. Place a damp jelly bag or several layers of cheesecloth in a strainer set over a bowl. Add the fruit mixture and strain for 6 to 8 hours. For clear juice, do not press the bag.
3. Pour the juice into a large pot or Dutch oven and add the sugar. Cook over medium heat, stirring to dissolve the sugar. Set the heat to high stirring constantly.
4. Cook and stir until the jelly reaches the gelling point. Use the plate method described here to check for gelling or use a digital thermometer. It should be 8 degrees above the boiling point of water, or about 220°F. This could take anywhere from 15 to 30 minutes. Detach from the heat and skim off the foam if necessary.
5. Ladle into 2 sterilized half-pints jar, leaving ¼-inch headspace. Top with two-piece lids and rings and close until finger-tight. Set in a water bath canner for 5 minutes.

Nutrition:

Calories: 159

Carbs: 34.8 g

Fiber: 7.2 g

Sugar: 8.8 g

Protein: 5.6 g

25. Strawberry Cabernet Black Pepper Jam

Preparation time: 15 minutes

Cooking time: 20 to 50 minutes

Servings: 2 pints jar

Ingredients:

- 1-pound fresh strawberries, cleaned and hulled
- 1½ cups granulated sugar
- 2 tablespoons bottled lemon juice
- 2 tablespoons cabernet sauvignon
- 1 teaspoon fresh cracked black pepper

Directions:

1. In a 3-quart saucepan, crush the strawberries with a potato masher.
2. Add the sugar, lemon juice, wine, and pepper. Set the mixture to a boil stirring until the sugar is dissolved.

3. Turn the heat up a little and cook rapidly, stirring often to prevent sticking, until the jam reaches the gelling point, which can take anywhere from 15 to 45 minutes. Use the plate method described here to check for gelling or use a digital thermometer; it should be 8 degrees above the boiling point of water, or about 220°F.
4. Ladle into 2 clean half-pints jar, leaving ¼-inch headspace. Top with two-piece lids and rings and close until finger-tight. Set in a water bath canner for 15 minutes, plus your altitude adjustment. Store in a dark, cool place. Jam is best eaten within 2 years.

Nutrition:

Calories: 102

Carbs: 7g

Fat: 6g

Protein: 1g

Chapter 4. Pickles

26. Bread and Butter Pickles

Preparation time: 30 minutes   **Cooking time:** 20 minutes   **Servings:** 8-9 pints jar

Ingredients:

- 15 cups sliced pickling cucumbers - about 6 lbs.
- 7 cups onions sliced thinly
- ¼ cup pickling salt
- 4 cups cider vinegar
- 4 ½ cups sugar
- ¾ tsp. turmeric
- ½ tsp. celery seed
- 1 Tbsp. mustard seeds

Directions:

1. Mix the onions, salt, and cucumbers together in a bowl. Cover with 2-inch crushed or cubed ice.
2. Bring a plate on top of the bowl with a gallon of water or something heavy on the plate. This serves as a weight. Let it stand for about 4 hours in the fridge.
3. After 4 hours, rinse, and drain the cucumbers very well.
4. Mix the sugar, vinegar, celery seed, mustard seed, and turmeric together in a large pot. Let boil for 10 minutes.
5. Add the drained cucumbers and slowly reheat to boiling.
6. Right at boiling, remove from heat, and fill the sanitized jars with slices and cooking syrup, leaving ½-inch headspace.
7. Adjust lids and process the jars in a hot water bath for 10 minutes.
8. Heat the water enough to maintain 180 to 185°F water temperature for 30 minutes. Check with a jelly thermometer to be certain that the water temperature is at least 180°F during the entire 30 minutes.

Nutrition:

Calories: 70   Fat: 3g

Carbs: 8g   Protein: 5g

27. Just-Right Dill Pickles

Preparation time: 10 minutes, plus overnight sitting time   **Cooking time:** 20 minutes   **Servings:** 8 pints jar

Ingredients:

- 6 pounds (3- to 4-inch) pickling cucumbers, washed and drained
- 1 cup pickling salt, divided
- 7 cups water, plus more as needed, divided
- 4 teaspoons mustard seed, divided
- 4 teaspoons dill seed, divided
- 4 garlic cloves, peeled, divided
- 2 tablespoons mixed pickling spice
- 5 cups white vinegar (5% acidity)
- ½ cup granulated sugar

Directions:

1. Slice ⅛ inch off the blossom ends of the cucumbers. The blossom end is usually smaller and has a rough dot as opposed to the larger, smoother dot on the stem end.
2. In a bowl or nonreactive pot, dissolve ¾ cup of salt in 2 cups of water. Add the cucumbers, then pour in enough water to cover the cucumbers. Cover and let sit overnight, either on the counter or in the refrigerator.
3. Drain and rinse the cucumbers. Slice each one in half lengthwise.
4. Pack 4 clean quart jars with the halved cucumbers, leaving ½-inch headspace. Add 1 teaspoon mustard seed, 1 teaspoon dill seed, and 1 garlic clove to each jar.

5. Tie the mixed pickling spice in a spice bag or piece of cheesecloth and put it in a large pot or Dutch oven. Add the vinegar, sugar, remaining ¼ cup of salt, and remaining 5 cups water and set to a boil. Set the heat and simmer for 15 minutes.

6. Discard the spice bag. Ladle the vinegar mixture over the cucumbers in the jars, leaving ½-inch headspace. Top with two-piece lids and rings and close until finger-tight. Set in a water bath canner for 15 minutes, plus your altitude adjustment.

Nutrition:

Calories: 170

Fat: 3g

Carbs: 23g

Protein: 14g

28. Gingery Gherkins

Preparation time: 20 minutes, plus 8 hours sitting time

Cooking time: 20 minutes

Servings: 6 pints jar

Ingredients:

- 4 pounds (2- to 3-inch) pickling cucumbers, washed and drained
- 4 garlic cloves, peeled, divided
- 4 teaspoons dill seed, divided
- 4 whole black peppercorns, divided
- 4 tablespoons peeled, chopped fresh ginger, divided
- 3 cups apple cider vinegar (5% acidity)
- 2 cups water
- ½ cup granulated sugar
- ⅓ cup pickling salt
- 1 cinnamon stick

Directions:

1. Slice ⅛ inch off the blossom ends of the cucumbers. The blossom end is usually smaller and has a rough dot as opposed to the larger, smoother dot on the stem end. Put the cucumbers in a large bowl. Secure them with boiling water and let sit for 8 to 12 hours at room temperature.

2. Drain the cucumbers and pierce each with a fork. Pack into 4 clean pints jar, leaving ½-inch headspace. Attach 1 garlic clove, 1 teaspoon dill seed, 1 peppercorn, and 1 tablespoon chopped ginger to each jar.

3. In a nonreactive pot over medium-high heat, combine the vinegar, water, sugar, salt, and cinnamon stick. Set until the sugar and salt have dissolved, reduce the heat, and simmer for 15 minutes.

4. Discard the cinnamon stick. Ladle the vinegar mixture over the cucumbers in the jars, leaving ½-inch headspace. Top with two-piece lids and rings and close until finger-tight. Set in a water bath canner for 15 minutes, plus your altitude adjustment.

Nutrition:

Calories: 215

Fat: 3g

Carbs: 35g

Protein: 15g

29. Giant Cucumber Pickles

Preparation time: 20 minutes, plus 12 hours sitting time

Cooking time: 20 minutes

Servings: 6 pints jar

Ingredients:

- 4 to 6 large, overripe cucumbers
- ¼ cup pickling salt
- 4 cups water
- 2 cups granulated sugar
- 1½ cups apple cider vinegar (5% acidity)
- ¾ cup water
- 1 cinnamon stick
- 2 teaspoons whole cloves
- 1 tablespoon mustard seed

Directions:

1. Peel the cucumbers. Set in half lengthwise and scoop out the seeds. Cut the pieces in half lengthwise again. If the pieces are too long to fit in a quart jar, cut them crosswise. You should have about 12 cups of cucumber pieces.
2. In a pot or Dutch oven, combine the salt and water. Stir until the salt dissolves.
3. Add the cucumber pieces to the pot. Let stand for at least 12 hours. Drain and rinse the cucumbers.
4. In a nonreactive pot, merge the sugar, vinegar, water, cinnamon stick, cloves, and mustard seed. Bring to a boil over medium-high heat. Add the drained cucumbers. Boil gently until the cucumbers are transparent, about 15 minutes.
5. Discard the cinnamon stick. Pack the strips into 3 clean pints jar. Ladle the vinegar mixture over the cucumbers in the jars, leaving ½-inch headspace. Top with two-piece lids and rings and close until finger-tight. Set in a water bath canner for 10 minutes.

Nutrition:

Calories: 50

Carbs: 2g

Fat: 0g

Protein: 10g

30. Zucchini Bread-and-Butter Pickles

Preparation time: 20 minutes, plus 2 hours sitting time

Cooking time: 5 minutes

Servings: 3 pints jar

Ingredients:

- 1 large onion, peeled and thinly sliced
- ⅓ cup pickling salt
- 2 cups apple cider vinegar (5% acidity)
- 1¼ cups granulated sugar
- 1 tablespoon mustard seed
- 1 teaspoon ground turmeric
- 1 teaspoon celery seed
- 1 teaspoon whole black peppercorns

Directions:

1. In a large bowl, merge the zucchini and onion slices. Set with the salt and cover with ice cubes. Let sit at room temperature for 2 hours. Drain and rinse well.
2. In a nonreactive pot or Dutch oven, combine the vinegar, sugar, mustard seed, turmeric, celery seed, and peppercorns. Bring to a boil over medium-high heat. Add the drained cucumber and onion slices and return to a boil.
3. Pack the cucumber and onion slices into 3 clean pints jar, leaving ½-inch headspace. Top with two-piece lids and rings and close until finger-tight. Set in a water bath canner for 10 minutes, plus your altitude adjustment.

Nutrition:

Calories: 314

Sodium: 73mg

Fat: 5.1g

Carbs: 1.3g

31. Pickled Baby Carrots

Preparation time: 10 minutes

Cooking time: 5 minutes

Servings: 2 pints jar

Ingredients:

- 1 pound baby carrots (about ½ inch thick and 2 to 6 inches long)
- 1 tablespoon plus ½ cup water, divided
- 4 bay leaves, divided
- 2 teaspoons whole black peppercorns, divided
- 2 strips lemon peel, divided
- 1¾ cups white vinegar (5% acidity)
- ½ cup bottled lemon juice
- ¼ cup granulated sugar
- 1 teaspoon pickling salt

Directions:

1. In a microwave-safe bowl, merge the carrots and 1 tablespoon of water, secure with a paper towel, and set on high for 2 to 5 minutes, until crisp-tender. Rinse with cold water.

2. Fill 2 clean pint canning jars with the carrots. Add 2 bay leaves, 1 teaspoon peppercorns, and 1 lemon strip to each jar.
3. In a medium nonreactive pan, bring the vinegar, lemon juice, remaining ½ cup of water, sugar, and salt to a simmer until the sugar dissolves. Reduce the heat to a simmer.
4. Ladle the vinegar mixture over the carrots in the jars, leaving ½-inch headspace. Top with two-piece lids and rings and close until finger-tight. Set in a water bath canner for 15 minutes, plus your altitude adjustment.

Nutrition:

Calories: 148

Fat: 2g

Carbs: 5.1g

Protein: 25.5g

32. Celery Seed Pickled Asparagus

Preparation time: 10 minutes   **Cooking time:** 5 minutes   **Servings:** 6 pints jar

Ingredients:

- 5½ pounds asparagus spears, washed and trimmed
- 6 garlic cloves, peeled, divided
- 5⅓ cups apple cider vinegar (5% acidity)
- 1⅓ cups water
- ⅓ cup pickling salt
- 2 tablespoons granulated sugar
- 1½ tablespoons celery seed
- 1 tablespoon mustard seed
- 2 teaspoons whole black peppercorns

Directions:

1. Trim the asparagus to lengths about 1 inch shorter than a three-quarter-pint jar. Tip 6 clean jars on their sides and pack with the asparagus. Add 1 garlic clove to each jar.
2. In a medium nonreactive pan, bring the vinegar, water, salt, sugar, celery seed, mustard seed, and peppercorns to a boil, stirring until the sugar and salt dissolve. Reduce the heat to a simmer while filling the jars.
3. Ladle the vinegar mixture over the asparagus in the jars, leaving ½-inch headspace. Top with two-piece lids and rings and close until finger-tight. Set in a water bath canner for 10 minutes, plus your altitude adjustment.

Nutrition:

Calories: 96

Fat: 1.7g

Carbs: 0g

Protein: 20.08g

33. Basil Garlic Pickled Beans

Preparation time: 10 minutes   **Cooking time:** 5 minutes   **Servings:** 3 pints jar

Ingredients:

- 1-pound green beans, washed and trimmed
- 3 garlic cloves, peeled, divided
- 9 fresh basil leaves, divided
- 1 cup water
- 2½ cups white vinegar (5% acidity)
- 3 tablespoons pickling salt
- 1 teaspoon red pepper flakes

Directions:

1. Pack the beans into 3 clean wide-mouth pints jar. Add 1 garlic clove and 3 basil leaves to each jar.
2. In a nonreactive saucepan, bring the water, vinegar, salt, and red pepper flakes to a boil, stirring until the salt dissolves.
3. Ladle the vinegar mixture over the beans in the jars, leaving ½-inch headspace. Top with two-piece lids and rings and close until finger-tight. Set in a water bath canner for 10 minutes, plus your altitude adjustment.

Nutrition:

Calories: 70

Carbs: 8g

Fat: 3g

Protein: 5g

34. Jalapeño Pickle

Preparation time: 15 minutes   **Cooking time:** 15 minutes   **Servings:** 8 pints jar

Ingredients:

- 6–8 pounds jalapeño peppers
- 5 cups vinegar
- 1 cup water
- 2 garlic cloves, crushed lightly
- 2 tablespoons sugar
- 4 teaspoons pickling salt

Directions:

1. Remove the stem end of each jalapeño pepper.
2. Cut the peppers into ¼–½-inch-thick rings.
3. In a large nonreactive saucepan, add the vinegar, water, garlic, sugar, and salt over medium-high heat and cook until boiling.
4. Cook for about 10 minutes.
5. Remove the saucepan of vinegar mixture from heat and discard the garlic.
6. In the bottom of 9 (1-pint) hot sterilized jars, divide the jalapeño rings.
7. Pour the hot vinegar mixture over the jalapeños, leaving about ½-inch space from the top.
8. Slide a small knife around the insides of each jar to remove air bubbles.
9. Close each jar with a lid and screw on the ring.
10. Arrange the jars in a boiling water canner and process for about 10 minutes.
11. Remove the jars from water canner and place onto a wood surface several inches apart to cool completely.

Nutrition:

Calories: 30

Fat: 0.1g

Carbs: 4.6g

Fiber: 2g

Protein: 0.7g

35. Dilled Beans Pickle

Preparation time: 10 minutes   **Cooking time:** 20 minutes   **Servings:** 6 pints jar

Ingredients:

- 3½ lb. yellow or green beans (Fresh)
- 5 cups White vinegar (5% acidity)
- 2 cups Water
- ⅓ cup Ball® Salt for Pickling & Preserving
- 1½ tsp. red pepper (dried and crushed)
- 12 dill sprigs (Fresh)
- 6 Garlic cloves (peeled and crushed)
- Ball® Pickle Crisp (optional)

Directions:

1. Before processing the beans, wash them, trim the ends of the stem, and cut them into pieces 4 inches in length.
2. Take a 3L Stainless Steel saucepan and add vinegar, water, Ball Salt, and red pepper. Allow it to boil.
3. Take a hot jar and add a crushed garlic clove and dill sprigs and pack whole beans in a jar.
4. Transfer the pickling liquid over beans in the jar with a ladle over the rind mixture. Leave ½ inch space on the top. If desired, add Ball® Pickle Crisp in the jar. Remove air bubbles. Clean the rim of the glass jar. Place the lid and apply a band around it. Adjust to ensure that the lid is tight. Set the jar in the water bath canner that has boiling water.
5. Leave the water bath canner for about 10 minutes.
6. Turn off the canner, remove the lid. Keep the jars in the canner for 5 minutes more.
7. Remove the jars and allow them to cool. Store in the refrigerator.

Nutrition:

Calories: 202

Fat: 2.3 g

Carbs: 31.4 g

Protein: 14.8 g

Fiber: 12.6 g

36. Onions and Peppers Pickle

Preparation time: 10 minutes   **Cooking time:** 20 minutes   **Servings:** 6 pints jar

Ingredients:

- 2 cups red onions (thick vertically sliced)
- 4 cups White vinegar (5% acidity)
- 4 cups Water
- 1½ cups Sugar
- ½ cup Ball® Salt
- 2 tsp. red pepper (dried and crushed)
- 2 Medium-sized Red Bell pepper (diced in thick strips)
- 2 Medium-sized yellow bell peppers (diced in thick strips)
- 2 Large-sized green bell peppers (diced in thick strips)
- ⅛ tsp. Ball® Pickle Crisp

Directions:

1. Before processing, take a bowl filled with ice water and soak onion slices into it for about 10 minutes.
2. Take a 2 Quarts Stainless Steel Saucepan and add vinegar, water, sugar, salt, and red pepper on medium-high flame. Stir continuously until sugar dissolves.
3. Drain the slices of onion and pat dry. Mix bell peppers and onions.
4. Transfer all the vegetables to the hot jar and pack them tightly. Add Pickle Crisp if desired. Leave½ inch space on the top. Remove air bubbles. Clean the rim of the glass jar. Place the lid and apply a band around it. Adjust to ensure that the lid is tight. Set the jar in the water bath canner that has boiling water.
5. Leave the water bath canner for about 10 minutes.
6. Turn off the canner, remove the lid. Keep the jars in the canner for 5 minutes more.

Nutrition:

Calories: 250

Carbs: 0g

Fat: 19g

Protein: 19g

37. Cabbage and Pepper Pickle

Preparation time: 15 minutes   **Cooking time:** 25 minutes   **Servings:** 6 pints jar

Ingredients:

- 2 pounds cabbage, cored and shredded
- 5 cups bell peppers, seeded and cut into thin strips
- ¼ cup pickling salt
- 1½ cups white wine vinegar
- 1 cup sugar
- 6 garlic cloves, minced
- 4 teaspoons mustard seeds
- ½ teaspoon hot pepper flakes

Directions:

1. In a glass bowl, add cabbage, bell peppers, and salt and mix well.
2. Cover the bowl and place in a cool place for about 8–12 hours.
3. Rinse the cabbage and drain completely.
4. In the bowl of cabbage mixture, add the garlic, mustard seeds, and red pepper flakes and toss to coat well.
5. In a nonreactive saucepan, add the vinegar and sugar and cook until boiling.
6. In the bottom of 4 (1-pint) hot sterilized jars, divide the cabbage mixture. Pour the vinegar mixture over the cabbage mixture, leaving about ½-inch space from the top.
7. Slide a small knife around the insides of each jar to remove air bubbles.
8. Close each jar with a lid and screw on the ring.
9. Process in water bath canner for about 20 minutes.

Nutrition:

Calories: 83
Fat: 0.4g

Carbs: 18.5g
Protein: 1.4g

38. Watermelon Style Pickles

Preparation time: 15 Minutes | **Cooking time:** 21 Hours and 15 minutes | **Servings:** 12 pints jar

Ingredients:

- 1cup salt, canning variety
- 1-gallon water, cold
- 16 cups watermelon Rind, cut into cubes
- 1-gallon water, cold
- Sticks cinnamon
- 1 teaspoon Allspice, whole
- 1 teaspoon cloves, whole
- 2 cups vinegar, white
- 2 cups sugar, white
- 12 Cherries, Maraschino Variety and cut into halves
- 6, 1 Pint Canning Jars, with and rings

Directions:

1. Stir your salt into your gallon of water in a large-sized container until it is completely dissolved. Add your watermelon rind, cover with some plastic wrap, and sit for the next 12 hours. After this time, drain and rinse completely.
2. Next, place your remaining gallon of water and watermelon rind into a large-sized stockpot. Set to a parboil.
3. Add your next 3 ingredients into a spice bag and submerge into your pot.
4. Add all your remaining ingredients and stir to combine.
5. After this time, remove your spice bag and remove your mixture from heat. Allow cooling completely.
6. Pour the mixture into your canning jars and seal with your lids.
7. Process in water bath canner for 10 minutes.

Nutrition:

Calories: 170
Carbs: 23g

Fat: 3g
Protein: 14g

39. Garlic Flavored Pickles

Preparation time: 5 minutes | **Cooking time:** 8 Hours and 5 minutes | **Servings:** 2 pints jar

Ingredients:

- 16 oz. jar pickles, dill variety
- 2 cups sugar, white
- 1tablespoon hot sauce, your favorite kind
- 6 garlic cloves, peeled and minced
- ¼ teaspoons red pepper flakes, crushed

Directions:

1. Place your canned dill pickles and the liquid into a large-sized bowl.
2. Add your remaining ingredients and stir thoroughly to combine.
3. Pour your mixture into your pickle jar and seal with your lid.
4. Process in water bath canning for the next 10 minutes.

Nutrition:

Calories: 50
Carbs: 2g

Fat: 0g
Protein: 10g

40. Garlic Dill Pickles

Preparation time: 5 Minutes | **Cooking time:** 30 Minutes | **Servings:** 6 pints jar

Ingredients:

- 10 cucumbers
- 2 cups vinegar
- 2 cups water
- 2 tablespoons salt

- 2 tablespoons dill seeds
- 6 garlic cloves
- 2 teaspoons peppercorns

Directions:
1. Chop the cucumbers.
2. Combine the vinegar, water, and salt and boil.
3. Separate the garlic, dill seeds, and peppercorns equally between the jars.
4. Pack the cucumbers tightly into the jars.
5. Pour the hot liquid into the jars.
6. Set in a boiling-water bath for 10 minutes.

Nutrition:

Calories: 202

Fat: 2.3 g

Carbs: 31.4 g

Fiber: 12.6 g

Protein: 14.8 g

41. Pickled Beets

Preparation time: 15 Minutes   **Cooking time:** 2 Hours   **Servings:** 4 pints jar

Ingredients:

- 6 beets
- 2 cups sugar
- ½ cups vinegar

- ½ cups water
- 1 tablespoon salt
- ¼ cup cloves

Directions:
1. Cover the chopped beets in water and cook for 30 minutes, until soft.
2. Combine the sugar, water, cloves, and vinegar and boil for 10 minutes.
3. Fill the beets into jars and pour boiling water on top.
4. Set in boiling water canner for 10 minutes.

Nutrition:

Calories: 250

Fat: 19g

Carbs: 0g

Protein: 19g

42. Pickled Peppers

Preparation time: 5 Minutes   **Cooking time:** 10 Minutes   **Servings:** 3 pints jar

Ingredients:

- 4 cups white vinegar
- 2 cups water
- 2 tablespoons sugar
- Olive oil
- Onion, medium diced

- Medium-sized carrots, medium diced
- Peppers
- Dried oregano
- Bay leaves

Directions:
1. Merge the water, vinegar and sugar in a medium saucepan and heat until the mixture reaches a simmer.
2. Meanwhile, sauté the carrots and onions in olive oil until tender.
3. Using pintsized canning jars, place approximately 1 tablespoon of your mixture in the bottom of a jar, then add the peppers (if you make 2 small incisions on each pepper, the flavors of the brine will infuse more quickly).
4. Add ½ teaspoon of oregano and one bay leaf to each jar. Seal the jars, and process in a hot water bath for 10 minutes.

Nutrition:

Calories: 170

Carbs: 23g

Fat: 3g

Protein: 14g

43. Chunky Zucchini Pickles

Preparation time: 15 Minutes   **Cooking time:** 35 Minutes   **Servings:** 15 pints jar

Ingredients:

- 14 cups unpeeled zucchini (I peeled half of them because this zucchini was huge and the skin was tougher than smaller zucchini)
- 6 cups finely chopped onions
- ¼ cup pickling or canning salt
- 3 cups granulated sugar
- 4 tablespoons Clearjel
- ¼ cup dry mustard
- 1 tablespoon ground ginger
- 1 teaspoon ground turmeric
- ½ cup water
- 2 cups white vinegar
- 1 red bell pepper

Directions:

1. In a stainless steel or glass bowl, merge the onions and zucchini. Sprinkle with pickling salt, cover, and allow to stand at room temperature for 1 hour
2. Prepare for water bath canning. Sterilize your jars in the oven at 250 °F for 30 minutes.
3. Combine the sugar, Clearjel, or corn starch, mustard, ginger, and turmeric in a large stainless-steel saucepan. Stir dry the ingredients well. Gradually blend in water. Add vinegar and red pepper.
4. Set to a boil frequently stirring to dissolve sugar and prevent lumps from forming. Reduce the heat and boil gently, frequently stirring, until the mixture thickens about 6 minutes. Add the zucchini mixture and return to a boil.
5. Ladle the hot zucchini mixture into hot sterilized jars, leaving right ½ headspace. Remove air bubbles and adjust headspace, if need it, by adding some more hot zucchini mixture. Wipe the rim with a damp towel. Place rings and snaps on each jar, screwing bands down until they are fingertip tight.
6. Place the jars in a canner, making sure they are completely covered with water. Bring to a full rolling boil and process for 10 minutes. When time is completed, turn off the heat, remove the canner lid and wait 6 minutes before removing jars to a folded clean towel on the counter.

Nutrition:

Calories: 202

Fat: 2.3 g

Carbs: 31.4 g

Fiber: 12.6 g

44. Mustard Pickled Vegetables

Preparation time: 15 Minutes   **Cooking time:** 15 Minutes   **Servings:** 4 pints jar

Ingredients:

- 1 head cauliflower
- 20 small green tomatoes
- 3 green bell peppers
- 4 cups pickling onions
- 2 pickling cucumbers
- 1 cup sugar
- ¾ cup flour
- ½ cup dry mustard
- 1 tablespoon turmeric
- 7 cups apple cider vinegar
- 7 cups water
- 1 cup pickling salt

Directions:

1. Wash all the veggies and chop them.
2. Toss the vegetables in a large nonreactive bowl or pot with salt.
3. Pour a quart of water over all of them and let this stand overnight.
4. Drain, secure with boiling water and let it stand for 10 minutes. Drain.
5. Combine the sugar, flour, spices, vinegar, and 3 cups of water, then cook until thick.

6. Merge in the veggies and cook until tender-crisp.
7. Pack into pints jar, dividing liquid evenly and leaving ½ inch of headspace.
8. Wipe rims, screw-on lids, and rings.
9. Finish the canning process in a boiling water bath for 15 minutes.

Nutrition:

Calories: 70

Carbs: 8g

Fat: 3g

Protein: 5g

45. Tarragon Pickled Green Beans

Preparation time: 15 Minutes   **Cooking time:** 2 Hours   **Servings:** 6 pints jar

Ingredients:

- 6 garlic cloves, thinly sliced
- 36 whole peppercorns, crushed
- 3 lbs. green beans, washed and trimmed to 4 inches
- 6 sprigs fresh tarragon (can be substituted with 12 basil sprigs)

- 3 ½ cups white wine vinegar, or just white vinegar
- 3 ½ cups water
- 2 tablespoons pickling salt or Kosher salt

Directions:

1. Process the lids.
2. Then, divide the garlic and peppercorns into 6-pints jar.
3. Pack the green beans into the jars tightly and add sprigs of tarragon/basil
4. Heat the water, vinegar, and salt to boil at medium heat. Pour over the green beans in your jars, give it ½ inch headspace.
5. Process for 5 minutes in boiling water. Remove and let cool. You should hear the ping as it cools.

Nutrition:

Calories: 50

Carbs: 2g

Fat: 0g

Protein: 10g

46. Pickled Curry Cauliflower

Preparation time: 5 Minutes   **Cooking time:** 45 Minutes   **Servings:** 4 pints jar

Ingredients:

- 1 ½ tablespoon canning salt
- 4 cups vinegar
- 3 cups water
- 3 teaspoons cumin seeds

- 3 teaspoons turmeric
- 3 teaspoons curry powder
- 5 lbs. cauliflower
- 6 Serrano peppers

Directions:

1. With a 4-quart kettle, combine the water, salt, and vinegar. Set to a simmer over low heat and whisk to help dissolve the salt. Keep hot until ready to use.
2. Pack jars with cauliflower. Add ½ teaspoon of cumin seeds, turmeric, and curry flower, and 1 Serrano pepper into each jar.
3. Pour hot brine into the jars, leaving ½ inch headspace.
4. Process for 12 minutes.

Nutrition:

Calories: 96

Fat: 1.7g

Carbs: 0g

Protein: 20.08g

47. Spicy Dill Pickles

Preparation time: 15 Minutes   **Cooking time:** 1 Hour   **Servings:** 6 pints jar

Ingredients:

- ½ teaspoon red pepper flakes
- 10 garlic cloves, peeled and smashed
- 5 teaspoons dill seed, separated
- 2 tablespoons canning salt
- 3 tablespoons honey
- 4 cups water
- 1cup white vinegar
- 3 cups apple cider vinegar
- 11 lbs. cucumber

Directions:

1. Combine both kinds of vinegar, honey, salt, and water. Set to a boil, then reduce to a simmer.
2. Cut ½ inch off each end of the cucumbers and discard. Slice ¼ inch slices and set aside. If you are not using fresh cucumber, soak in ice water for 2 hours first.
3. Add one smashed garlic clove and one hot pepper or ½ red pepper flakes in each jar. Pack cucumbers in, give it ½ inch headspace. Add ½ teaspoon of dill seed on top.
4. Pour brine over, giving the same headspace.
5. Set jars in boiling water for 10 minutes.

Nutrition:

Calories: 170

Carbs: 23g

Fat: 3g

Protein: 14g

48. Spiced Beets

Preparation time: 5 Minutes   **Cooking time:** 60 Minutes   **Servings:** 4 pints jar

Ingredients:

- ¼ teaspoon salt
- ¾ teaspoon allspice
- ¾ teaspoon cloves
- ¼ stick cinnamon
- ¼ piece mace
- 1 ½ teaspoon celery seed
- 2 cups cider vinegar, 5% acidity
- 1 cup sugar
- 2 pints beets

Directions:

1. Sterilize a quart jar for 15 minutes. Remove your jar from the water and pour in the vinegar mix. Fix the lid and set it aside for 2 weeks.
2. Remove the spice bag. Cook fresh beets until tender but firm and let cool. Peel the beets. Heat the vinegar and add ½ cup of the beet liquid. Add the beets and simmer for 15 minutes.
3. Pack into sterile jars, being sure the vinegar covers the beets. Remove air bubbles and adjust the lids. Process for 10 minutes in a boiling water bath.

Nutrition:

Calories: 70

Carbs: 8g

Fat: 3g

Protein: 5g

49. Pickled Asparagus

Preparation time: 10 minutes   **Cooking time:** 20 minutes   **Servings:** 6 pints jar

Ingredients:

- 1 clove of garlic
- Organic red pepper flakes, ½ teaspoon
- Sea salt to taste (about ¼ teaspoon)
- Mustard seeds, one teaspoon
- Dried oregano, one teaspoon
- 1 teaspoon of organic dill
- Black peppercorns, ½ teaspoon
- 16-20 spears of fresh asparagus (local and organic is preferred) and even in size
- 1 cup of water
- 1 cup of vinegar (white vinegar)

Directions:

1. Prepare the mason jar (or jars, if a double or larger batch is made) by cleaning them with soap and warm water, then boiling the jars and lids in water for up to 15 minutes. Bring the jars on the counter on a towel. Place the garlic, red pepper flakes, dill seeds, sea salt, dried oregano, black peppercorns, and mustard seeds in each of the jars.
2. Wash the asparagus thoroughly and trim the stems off each so that they can adequately fit into each of the jars without having to fold them.
3. Fill each of the jars with as many asparagus spears, evenly distributing them, making sure each jar, if multiple is prepared, have the same number of spears in each.
4. In a small or medium saucepan, attach the vinegar and water and bring to a boil.
5. This will create the brine to pour over the asparagus. You may necessarily to change the amounts depending on how many jars are processed. Once the brine is boiled and ready, pour gently into each of the prepared jars, filling over the asparagus and other ingredients inside until there is only ¼ inch of space at the top.
6. Lay a lid on top of each jar and secure tightly.
7. Allow the jars to cool at room temperature, then refrigerate to use within one month. For longer storage, place the prepared and sealed jars in a water bath canner for 15 minutes, with the water covering at least one inch over the tops of the jars, then gently remove and cool overnight on a wire rack.
8. Once cooled, store in your pantry or a fruit cellar for up to one year.

Nutrition:

Carbohydrates: 3g

Fat: 0g

Protein: 0g

Sodium: 15mg

Calories: 13

50. Spicy Carrots

Preparation time: 5 Minutes   **Cooking time:** 60 Minutes   **Servings:** 4 pints jar

Ingredients:

- ¼ teaspoon salt
- ¾ teaspoon allspice
- ¾ teaspoon cloves
- ¼ stick cinnamon
- ¼ piece mace

- 1 ½ teaspoon celery seed
- 2 cups cider vinegar, 5% acidity
- 1 cup sugar
- 2 pints carrots

Directions:

1. Tie the salt and the spices in a thin cloth bag. Boil the vinegar, sugar, and spices for 15 minutes. Sterilize a quart jar for about 15 minutes in boiling water. Remove your jar from the water and pour in the vinegar mix. Fix the lid and set it aside for 2 weeks.
2. Remove the spice bag. Cook fresh carrots until tender but firm and let cool. Heat the vinegar and add ½ cup of the carrot liquid. Add the carrots and simmer for 15 minutes.
3. Pack into sterile jars, being sure the vinegar covers the carrots. Remove air bubbles and adjust the lids. Set 10 minutes in a boiling water bath.

Nutrition:

Calories: 170

Carbs: 23g

Fat: 3g

Protein: 14g

Chapter 5.   Fruits

51. Piña Colada Jelly

Preparation time: 15 Minutes   **Cooking time:** 25 Minutes   **Servings:** 2 pints jar

Ingredients:

- 1 pineapple, chopped
- ⅓ cup coconut cream
- 3 oz. pectin
- ¼ teaspoon butter
- 3 cups sugar
- ½ cup coconut

Directions:

1. Crush the pineapple and add it to a pot with the Pectin.
2. Pour the coconut cream, sugar, and butter over it.
3. Boil for 10 minutes.
4. Pour into your sterilized jars and process in a boiling-water canner for 5 minutes.

Nutrition:

Calories: 70

Carbs: 8g

Fat: 3g

Protein: 5g

52. Sweet Crabapple Jelly

Preparation time: 5 Minutes   **Cooking time:** 15 Minutes   **Servings:** 5 pints jar

Ingredients:

- 8 cups crabapples, fresh
- Some water, as needed
- 3 cups sugar, white
- 1, 3-inch cinnamon stick, optional

Directions:

1. Remove the stems and blossoms from your crabapples and then cut them into quarters. Place into a large-sized saucepan.
2. Add in some water to cover and bring to a boil over medium heat. Allow boiling for the next 10 to 15 minutes or until they are tender to the touch.
3. After this time, strain your apples and juice them. Discard any pulp and place your juice back into your pan.
4. Heat over low heat and allow to cook for the next 10 minutes. After this time, skim off any foam appeared on the top of your mixture.
5. Add in your sugar and stir thoroughly until completely dissolved.
6. Boil for the next 20 minutes before removing from heat. Allow cooling completely.
7. Pour the mixture into your canning jars and seal with your lids.
8. Process the water bath canner for the next 10 minutes. Remove and let it cool slightly before placing it into your fridge.

Nutrition:

Calories: 250

Fat: 19g

Carbs: 0g

Protein: 19g

53. Apple Banana Butter

Preparation time: 5 Minutes   **Cooking time:** 2 ½ Hours   **Servings:** 4 pints jar

Ingredients:

- 2 lbs. apples
- 3 bananas
- ¾ cup sugar
- 1 cup water

Directions:

1. Combine all the ingredients and cook for 2 hours.

2. Fill into jars.
3. Process in boiling water canner for 7 minutes.

Nutrition:

Calories: 83

Fat: 0.4g

Carbs: 18.5g

Protein: 1.4g

54. Apple Butter

Preparation time: 15 Minutes　　**Cooking time:** 45 Minutes　　**Servings:** 6 pints jar

Ingredients:

- 14 apples
- 2 cups water
- 3 cups sugar
- 3 teaspoons cinnamon

Directions:

1. Core, peel, and cut the apples.
2. Combine the apples with water and cook until soft. Puree.
3. Add the sugar and cinnamon.
4. Boil over medium heat until it thickens.
5. Ladle into your prepared jars and process in boiling water canner for 10 minutes.

Nutrition:

Calories: 170

Carbs: 23g

Fat: 3g

Protein: 14g

55. Banana Butter

Preparation time: 5 Minutes　　**Cooking time:** 30 Minutes　　**Servings:** 4 pints jar

Ingredients:

- 5 bananas
- 3 cups chopped pineapple
- ¼ cup desiccated coconut
- 3 cups sugar
- 5 teaspoons lemon juice
- ¼ cup water

Directions:

1. Merge all ingredients in a pot and bring to a boil.
2. Cook until the mixture thickens.
3. Transfer into jars.
4. Set in boiling water bath for 15 minutes.

Nutrition:

Calories: 170

Carbs: 23g

Fat: 3g

Protein: 14g

56. Hot Pepper Mustard Butter

Preparation time: 15 Minutes　　**Cooking time:** 1 Hour　　**Servings:** 9 pints jar

Ingredients:

- 35 large hot peppers
- 1 yellow bell pepper
- 1 big onion, trimmed and quartered
- 1-quart prepared yellow mustard
- 1quart cider vinegar
- 6 cups sugar
- 1 ¼ cup flour
- 1 ½ cups water
- 1 teaspoon salt

Directions:

1. Place the hot peppers, bell pepper, and onion in the food processor and pulse until finely minced.
2. Merge all the ingredients in a saucepan. Bring to a boil while stirring continuously. Set heat to low and let simmer for 20 minutes, stirring a few times.

3. Put into your hot sterilized jars, put the lids on, and allow them to sit in a water bath for about 10 minutes.
4. Let cool completely before storing.

Nutrition:

Calories: 170

Carbs: 23g

Fat: 3g

Protein: 14g

57. Blackberry Apple Jelly

Preparation time: 45 minutes   **Cooking time:** 20 minutes   **Servings:** 6 pints jar

Ingredients:

- 3 pounds blackberries (about 2½ quarts)
- 1¼ cups of water
- 7 to 8 medium apples
- Additional water
- Bottled apple juice, optional
- ¼ cup of bottled lemon juice
- 8 cups of sugar
- 2 pouches (3 ounces every) liquid fruit pectin

Directions:

1. Bring brown fruit and water to a boil Dutch oven. Slow to low heat and cook for 5 minutes. Set a sieve on a basin, bordered with four layers of cheesecloth. Place the berry mixture in the sieve and cover with cheesecloth.
2. Allow to strain for 30 minutes, retaining the juice and discarding the pulp. Take the stalks and finish of the apples and discard them (do not pare or core them); chop them into tiny pieces. Add just enough water to cover in the Dutch oven. Bring the water to a boil. Reduce heat for 20 minutes to low and cook. or until the apples are soft.
3. Using a cheesecloth-lined strainer, drain the juice while discarding the pulp. Return the blackberry and apple juices to the pan after measuring them. Add water or bottled apple juice to make 4 cups of if necessary. After that, add the lemon juice and sugar. On high heat, bring to a full rolling boil, stirring frequently.
4. Add the pectin and mix well. Boil for another minute, stirring frequently. Remove excess foam from heat and skim. Fill nine hot sterilized half-pints jar with the heated mixture, allowing ¼ inch headspace. Clean the rims. Screw on bands until fingertip tight; center lids on jars.
5. Place jars in simmering water in a canner, making sure they are well covered. Cook for 5 minutes and bring to boil. Remove and chill the jars. Remove them.

Nutrition:

Carbohydrates: 3g

Fat: 0g

Protein: 0g

Sodium: 15 mg

Calories: 13

58. Honeyed Oranges

Preparation time: 5 Minutes   **Cooking time:** 70 Minutes   **Servings:** 4 pints jar

Ingredients:

- 3 lbs. oranges
- 1 ½ cups sugar
- 1 ½ cups honey
- 5 teaspoons lemon juice
- Spices (cinnamon, cloves, nutmeg)

Directions:

1. Chop the oranges and combine, peel included, with water.
2. Set to a simmer and simmer for 20 minutes.
3. Combine the remaining ingredients in a separate pan.
4. Set to a boil, stirring until sugar is processed.
5. Add oranges and boil for 45 minutes.

6. Pour into boiling water canner and process for 15 minutes.

Nutrition:

Calories: 170

Carbs: 23g

Fat: 3g

Protein: 14g

59. Plums

Preparation time: 15 Minutes   **Cooking time:** 30 Minutes   **Servings:** 3 pints jar

Ingredients:

- 2 lbs. plums
- 2 ½ cups water
- 1 cup honey
- ½ cup orange juice
- 1 teaspoon cinnamon powder

Directions:

1. Combine water, honey, and orange juice.
2. Set to a boil and simmer for 5 minutes.
3. Add chopped plums and cinnamon powder to the mixture.
4. Boil until plums soften.
5. Fill the jars with the mixture.
6. Process in your boiling water canner for 15 minutes.

Nutrition:

Calories: 70

Carbs: 8g

Fat: 3g

Protein: 5g

60. Watermelon Jelly with Pectin

Preparation time: 5 Minutes   **Cooking time:** 31 Minutes   **Servings:** 8 pints jar

Ingredients:

- 12 cups cubed watermelon
- 3 tablespoons distilled white vinegar
- 5 cups sugar
- ½ cup bottled lemon juice
- 6 oz. pouches liquid pectin

Directions:

1. Cover the jars with hot water in a large pot, add 1 tablespoon of distilled white vinegar, and bring to a boil for 5 minutes.
2. Puree the watermelon in a food processor. Using the cheesecloth draining Direction, gently place the watermelon puree on the cheesecloth and drain for 30 minutes, or until you've captured 4 cups of juice.
3. Transfer the juice to a heavy-bottomed pot and add the sugar and lemon juice. Mix well.
4. Boil over high heat, constantly stirring. Once at a boil, add the liquid pectin and mix well.
5. Return to a boil and boil hard for 1 minute, constantly stirring. Remove from the heat. Discard the foam using a spoon.
6. Arrange the hot jars on a cutting board and ladle the hot jelly into the jars, leaving a ¼ inch headspace. Remove any air bubbles and add additional jelly if necessary to maintain the ¼ inch apart.
7. Clean each jar's rims with a warm washcloth dipped in distilled white vinegar.
8. Transfer the jars in the water bather, ensuring each jar is covered by at least 1 inch of water.
9. Attach 2 tablespoons of distilled vinegar to the water and adjust the heat to high.
10. Boil and process half-pints for 10 minutes.

Nutrition:

Calories: 50

Carbs: 2g

Fat: 0g

Protein: 10g

61. Canned Honey and Cinnamon Peaches

Preparation time: 15 Minutes   **Cooking time:** 5 Minutes   **Servings:** 4 pints jar

Ingredients:

- 3 lbs. ripe peaches
- 1 cup honey
- 7 cinnamon sticks

Directions:

1. Peel the peaches and dunk them in boiling water for 2 minutes. The skin will then come off.
2. Meanwhile, mix 9 cups of water and honey, and bring the mixture to a boil over medium heat.
3. Place a cinnamon stick in each sterilized pint jar. Pack the peaches in the jars and add the honey mixture, leaving some space.
4. Process the pints jar for 30 minutes in the boiling water.

Nutrition:

Calories: 170

Carbs: 23g

Fat: 3g

Protein: 14g

62. Pear Flavored Butter

Preparation time: 15 Minutes   **Cooking time:** 31 Minutes   **Servings:** 5 pints jar

Ingredients:

- 4 lbs. pears, medium in size, cored and cut into quarters
- 2 cups sugar, white
- 1 teaspoon orange zest, finely grated
- ¼ teaspoons nutmeg, ground
- ¼ cup orange juice, fresh

Directions:

1. Place your pears into a large pot placed over medium heat. Add water to cover your pears and cook until they are tender to the touch. This should take 30 minutes.
2. After this time, remove your pears and press through a sieve; hold onto your pulp.
3. Place your pear pulp into a large-sized saucepan along with your sugar and stir thoroughly until your sugar fully dissolves.
4. Add your remaining ingredients and cook this mixture over medium heat until it is a thick consistency. Cook for the next hour.
5. Pour the mixture into your canning jars and seal with your lids.
6. Boil the water bath canner for the next 10 minutes. Remove and let it cool slightly before placing it into your fridge. Use whenever you are ready.

Nutrition:

Calories: 56

Fat: 0g

Carbs: 13g

Protein: 1g

63. Simple Cranberry Butter

Preparation time: 5 Minutes   **Cooking time:** 20 Minutes   **Servings:** 1 pint jar

Ingredients:

- 2 tablespoons cranberries, dried
- ½ cup water, boiling
- ½ cup butter, soft to the touch
- 3 tablespoons sugar, Confectioner's Variety

Directions:

1. Stir your boiling water and cranberries in a large bowl. Allow steeping for the next 5 minutes.
2. After this time, drain your cranberries and chop them finely.
3. Then use an electric mixer and beat your butter in a separate medium-sized bowl until light and fluffy in texture.
4. Add your sugar and cranberries and beat until thoroughly combined.
5. Pour the mixture into your canning jars and seal with your lids.

6. Boil the jars in some boiling water for the next 10 minutes. Remove and let it cool slightly before placing it into your fridge. Use whenever you are ready.

Nutrition:

Calories: 82

Protein: 0g

Fiber: 0g

Fat: 0g

Carbs: 82g

64. Classic Banana Jam

Preparation time: 15 Minutes   **Cooking time:** 15 Minutes   **Servings:** 2 pints jar

Ingredients:

- 4 cups bananas, ripe
- ⅓ cup lemon juice, fresh

- 2 tablespoons brown sugar, light and packed
- ¼ teaspoons nutmeg, ground

Directions:

1. Attach all your ingredients into a blender and blend on the highest setting until smooth consistency.
2. Place into your canning jars and seal with your lids.
3. Boil the jars in some boiling water for the next 10 minutes. Remove and let it cool slightly before placing it into your fridge. Use whenever you are ready.

Nutrition:

Calories: 142

Protein: 0g

Fiber: 1g

Fat: 0g

Carbs: 36g

65. Acorn Squash Style Butter

Preparation time: 5 Minutes   **Cooking time:** 3 Hours   **Servings:** 6 pints jar

Ingredients:

- 3 acorn squashes, cut into halves and seeded
- 1 teaspoon cinnamon, ground
- 1 teaspoon nutmeg, ground
- 1 teaspoon ginger, ground

- ½ teaspoons cloves, ground
- ¼ cups brown sugar, light and packed
- 1 ½ ounce can apple Juice, concentrated, frozen, and thawed

Directions:

1. Preheat your oven to 400 °F.
2. Next, fill up 2 medium-sized baking dishes with at least 1 inch of water. Then place your sliced acorn squash into your baking pan and place it into your oven to bake until tender to the touch. This should take at least 1 hour. After this time, remove and discard your water. Set aside to cool completely.
3. Scoop the flesh out from your squash and add it into a blender. Blend on the highest setting until smooth in its consistency.
4. Add your next4 ingredients and blend again to combine until thick consistency.
5. Spoon into a large-sized saucepan. Add in your brown sugar and apple juice and continue to cook over medium heat for the next 40 to 45 minutes or until thick in its consistency.
6. Detach from heat and let it cool slightly.
7. Pour the mixture into your canning jars and seal with your lids.
8. Process the jars water bath for the next 10 minutes. Remove and let it cool slightly before placing it into your fridge. Use whenever you are ready.

Nutrition:

Calories: 104

Protein: 0g

Fiber: 0g

Fat: 1g

Carbs: 27g

66. Healthy Chia Seed Jam

Preparation time: 15 Minutes   **Cooking time:** 35 Minutes   **Servings:** 3 pints jar

Ingredients:

- ¼ cup chia seeds
- ½ cup water, cold
- 2 cups raspberries, frozen
- ½ cup blackberries, frozen
- ½ cup blueberries, frozen
- 2 strawberries, frozen
- ⅓ cup honey, raw

Directions:

1. Set your chia seeds in some water until it resembles a jelly-like consistency. This should take about 5 minutes.
2. Add your berries and honey into a medium-sized saucepan. Place over medium heat and cook until your berries are tender to the touch. This should take about 15 minutes.
3. After this time, crush your berries thoroughly until smooth consistency.
4. Next, stir your chia seed mixture into your berry mixture until thoroughly combined.
5. Detach from heat and let it cool slightly.
6. Pour the mixture into your canning jars and seal with your lids.
7. Boil the jars in some boiling water for the next 10 minutes. Remove and let it cool slightly before placing it into your fridge.

Nutrition:

Calories: 88

Protein: 0g

Fiber: 0g

Fat: 0g

Carbs: 23g

67. Budget-Friendly Berry Jam

Preparation time: 5 Minutes   **Cooking time:** 25 Minutes   **Servings:** 4 pints jar

Ingredients:

- 4 cups green tomato pulp
- 4 cups sugar, white
- 2-3 oz. jelly package, your favorite kind

Directions:

1. First, use a large-sized saucepan placed over medium to high heat. Add your tomato pulp and sugar and bring this mixture to a boil.
2. Once your mixture is boiling, set the heat to low and cook for the next 20 minutes, making sure you stir the mixture occasionally.
3. Remove your mixture from heat and add your jelly, making sure to stir thoroughly to combine and until it completely dissolves. Allow your mixture to cool completely.
4. Pour the mixture into your canning jars and seal with your lids.
5. Boil the jars in some boiling water for the next 10 minutes. Remove and let it cool slightly before placing it into your fridge.

Nutrition:

Calories: 314

Protein: 0.9g

Carbs: 81.1g

Fat: 0.2g

Sugar: 77.6g

68. Canning Oranges

Preparation time: 10 Minutes   **Cooking time:** 25 Minutes   **Servings:** 15 pints jar

Ingredients:

- 10½ cups of water
- 15 lb. of oranges, peeled & trimmed
- 1¼ cups of sugar

Directions:
1. Break the clean oranges into sections.
2. Add to the jars, packing tightly.
3. Mix the sugar in boiling water, stir to dissolve. Pour on top of the oranges, leaving half-inch space from above. Remove any air bubbles. Wipe the jar's rim, place the lid on top and screw the bands.
4. Bring the jars in the water bath canner for 10 minutes, adjust time according to the altitude.

Nutrition:

Calories: 43

Fat: 0g

Carbohydrates: 11.3g

Sugar: 11g

Protein: 0.1g

---

69. Fresh Tasting Papaya Jam

Preparation time: 5 Minutes | **Cooking time:** 5 Hours and 5 minutes | **Servings:** 5 pints jar

Ingredients:

- 5 cups papaya, ripped and mashed
- ¼ cup orange juice, fresh
- 1 ⅓ (1.75-ounce package) pectin, dry
- 5 cups sugar, white

Directions:
1. First, stir your first 3 ingredients in a large-sized pot placed over medium to high heat.
2. Once your mixture begins to boil, add in your sugar and constantly stir as it cooks.
3. Simmer for at least 2 to 3 minutes before removing from heat and allowing it to cool completely.
4. Pour the mixture into your canning jars and seal with your lids.
5. Boil the jars in some boiling water for the next 10 minutes. Remove and let it cool slightly before placing it into your fridge. Use whenever you are ready.

Nutrition:

Calories: 37

Protein: 1.9g

Carbs: 7.4g

Fat: 0.8g

Sugar: 1.3g

---

70. Simple Gooseberry Jam

Preparation time: 15 Minutes | **Cooking time:** 30 Minutes | **Servings:** 5 pints jar

Ingredients:

- 2 quarts gooseberries, fresh
- 6 cups sugar, white
- ½ (6-ounces container) pectin, liquid variety

Directions:
1. First, remove the blossom and stems from your gooseberries. Then puree your gooseberries until smooth consistency.
2. Place into a large-sized pot and add in your sugar.
3. Set this mixture to a boil over high heat and allow it to boil for at least one minute, making sure to stir as it boils constantly.
4. After this time, remove from heat and add in your pectin. Stir to combine. Make sure to skim off any foam from your mixture. Allow cooling completely.
5. Pour the mixture into your canning jars and seal with your lids.
6. Process the jars in water bath canner for the next 10 minutes. Remove and let it cool slightly before placing it into your fridge.

Nutrition:

Carbohydrates: 1g

Fat: 0g

Protein: 1g

Calories: 4g

Sodium: 727mg

71. Fresh Berries

Preparation time: 15 minutes   **Cooking time:** 25 minutes   **Servings:** 8 pints jar

Ingredients:

- 1 gallon (5.5 pounds) fresh berries
- 7 cups distilled or filtered water
- 7 tablespoons lemon juice

Directions:

1. Pour some lemon juice into the jar using the following ratio: 1 tablespoon for every pint-sized jar or 2 tablespoons for every quart-sized jar.
2. Add the berries to the jar. You should also discard mushy or soft berries.
3. Set the jars with water, leaving about ½ inch of space at the top.
4. Add the lids. Use the water bath canning method (30 minutes for quart-sized jars or 15 minutes for pint-sized jars) to seal the preserve the berries.

Nutrition:

Carbohydrates: 3g

Sodium: 11mg

Fat: 0g

Calories: 14

Protein: 1g

72. Applesauce

Preparation time: 15 minutes   **Cooking time:** 15 minutes   **Servings:** 16 pints jar

Ingredients:

- 21 pounds apples
- Sugar to taste
- Cinnamon to taste, optional

Directions:

1. Peel and core the apples. Set the apples in a large pot and set on the stove. Cook the apples over medium heat. If necessary, add 1 cup of water to help keep the apples from sticking.
2. Place a lid on the pot and let simmer until the apples are tender. Stir often throughout the simmering process.
3. Transfer the tender apples to a food process and blend until smooth.
4. Transfer the blended apples to a pot and place on the stove. Heat while adding sugar and cinnamon to taste.
5. Divide the applesauce evenly between the jars. Secure the lids on the jars and process using the water bathe canning method for 10 to 15 minutes.

Nutrition:

Calories: 122

Protein: 0g

Total fat: 0g

Sugars: 25g

Carbs: 32g

Fiber: 3g

73. Pears

Preparation time: 15 minutes   **Cooking time:** 15 minutes   **Servings:** 8 pints jar

Ingredients:

- 8 to 12 pounds pears (peeled, cored and halved)
- 2 ¼ cups sugar
- 5 ¼ cups water

Directions:

1. Make the syrup by merging the sugar with the water in a large saucepan. Set the mixture to a boil while stirring until the sugar has dissolved completely. Reduce the heat to keep the syrup warm.

2. Place the halved pears in a saucepan and warm over low heat.
3. Pack the warmed pears into the jars. Leave about ½ inch of headroom in each jar. Add the warm syrup to the jars leaving about ½ inch headroom in each jar.
4. Attach the lids in place and process using the water bath canning method for 20-25 minutes.

Nutrition:

Carbohydrates: 30g   Sodium: 225mg

Fat: 0g   Calories: 123

Protein: 1g

74. Peaches

Preparation time: 15 minutes   **Cooking time:** 10 minutes   **Servings:** 3 pints jar

Ingredients:

- 1 lb. bushel peaches, bleached and peeled
- 5 ¼ cups water
- 2 ¼ cups granulated sugar

Directions:

1. Mix the water with some sugar together in a saucepan. Bring the mixture to a simmer until the sugar has dissolved. This is the syrup that you will be canning the peaches in. You need to keep the syrup warm but not too hot that it cooks down.
2. Cut the bleached and peeled peaches in halves and remove the stone.
3. Fill the jars with the laved peaches and add some warm syrup to the jars. You want to leave about ½ inch space at the top of the jar.
4. Secure the lids on the jars before processing using the water bath canning method for 20 minutes.

Nutrition:

Calories: 68   Fat: 0.1g

Protein: 0.1g   Sugar: 10g

Carbs: 14g

75. Lime Jelly

Preparation time: 15 Minutes   **Cooking time:** 40 Minutes   **Servings:** 4 pints jar

Ingredients:

- 10 limes
- 2 cups water
- 4 cups sugar
- 3 oz. pectin

Directions:

1. Set the peel of the limes and squeeze the juice out of them.
2. Combine lime juice, peel, water, and sugar in a pan.
3. Bring to a rolling boil, constantly stirring.
4. And pectin and boil for 2 more minutes.
5. Ladle into jars and process in a boiling-water canner for 10 minutes.

Nutrition:

Carbohydrates: 1g   Sodium: 30mg

Fat: 0g   Calories: 3

Protein: 0g

Chapter 6.   Vegetables

76. Apricot Amaretto Jam

Preparation time: 30 minutes   **Cooking time:** 10 minutes   **Servings:** 8 half-pints

Ingredients:

- 4¼ cups peeled, crushed apricots
- ¼ cup lemon juice
- 6¼ cups erythritol, divided
- 1 package powdered fruit pectin
- ½ teaspoon unsalted butter
- ⅓ cup amaretto

Directions:

1. In a Dutch oven, merge lemon juice and apricots.
2. In a small bowl, merge pectin and ¼ cup erythritol. Stir into apricot mixture and add butter. Set to a full boil over medium-high heat, stirring constantly.
3. Stir in the remaining erythritol and let boil 1-2 minutes, stirring constantly.
4. Remove from heat and stir in amaretto.
5. Divide the hot mixture between 8 hot sterilized half-pints jar, leaving ¼-inch space of the top. Wipe the rims carefully. Set tops on jars and screw on bands until fingertip tight.
6. Set jars into canner with boiling water, ensuring that they are completely covered with water. Let boil for 10 minutes. Remove jars and cool.

Nutrition:

Carbohydrates: 21g

Fat: 0g

Protein: 0g

Cholesterol: 0mg

Sugar: 0g

Calories: 86

77. Tomato with Hot Pepper

Preparation time: 13 minutes   **Cooking time:** 45 minutes   **Servings:** 12 pints jar

Ingredients:

- 12 pounds (5.4 kg) of tomatoes, peeled and cut into chunks
- 3 bell peppers, diced
- 1 large onion, diced
- 2 pounds (907 g) diced hot peppers
- 1 cup white vinegar
- ¼ cup sugar
- 4 tablespoons chili powder
- 2 tablespoons canning salt
- 1 tablespoon lime juice per jar

Directions:

1. Set all the ingredients except for the lime juice into a large stockpot and stir to combine everything.
2. Place the mixture to a simmer and allow it to cook uncovered for 45 minutes to reduce the liquid and meld the delicious flavors.
3. Attach a tablespoon of lime juice to each pint jar then ladle in the super-yummy mixture, leaving ½ inch of headspace.
4. Pop the lids on and then process this in a water bath canner for 15 minutes, adjusting for altitude.

Nutrition:

Calories: 171

Total fat: 0g

Carbs: 44g

Protein: 0g

Sugars: 36g

Fiber: 2g

Sodium: 52mg

Potassium: 146mg

78. Mexican Tomato Sauce

Preparation time: 15 minutes   **Cooking time:** 1 hour & 25 minutes   **Servings:** 5 pints

Ingredients:

- 2 cups (2 Large) White onion, chopped
- 1 cup (250 mL) Chicken stock
- ⅓ cup (75 mL) Lemon Juice
- 2 tsp. Salt
- 4 ⅓ lb. Plum tomatoes, coarsely chopped
- 6 Garlic cloves, chopped
- ¼ cup Cilantro, fresh and chopped

Directions:

1. In a 6 Liter Stainless steel Dutch oven, mix white onion, chicken stock, lemon juice, salt, plum tomatoes, and garlic cloves.
2. Secure it and let it simmer for about 45 minutes or more on medium-low flame with frequent stirring. Detach from flame and allow it to cool.
3. Take a blender and process all the tomato mixture into a smooth paste. Strain the tomato paste using a fine wire mesh strainer in a large bowl.
4. Press the tomato mixture and remove any tomato peel or seeds from the paste and discard them.
5. Pour the strained tomato paste into a large skillet. Allow it to boil, reduce the flame, let it simmer until the tomato puree starts to thicken. Add cilantro and stir it well.
6. Transfer the hot sauce into a hot jar with a ladle. Leave ½ inch space on the top. Remove air bubbles. Clean the rim of the glass jar.
7. Place the lid and apply a band around it. Adjust to ensure that the lid is tight. Set the jar in the water bath canner that has boiling water.
8. Leave the water bath canner for about 40 minutes. Turn off the canner, remove the lid. Keep the jars in the canner for 5 minutes more.
9. Remove the jars and allow them to cool. Store in the refrigerator.

Nutrition:

Calories: 71

Carbs: 14g

Fat: 1g

Protein: 1g

79. Pickled Snap Pea with Carrot

Preparation time: 10 minutes **Cooking time:** 5 minutes **Servings:** 2 pints jar

Ingredients:

- 1½ lbs. sugar snap peas
- 1 julienned carrot
- 2 sliced jalapeño peppers
- 4 chopped garlic cloves
- 2 cups distilled white vinegar
- 1 cup water
- 2 tsps. canning salt

Directions:

1. Wash the pea pods, trim off the ends, and remove the stringy portion. Cut the pea pods into thirds, making bite-sized pieces.
2. Mix the chopped-up peas, carrots, jalapeños, and garlic.
3. In a medium-sized, nonreactive saucepan, boil water, vinegar and salt for 3 minutes.
4. Fill the prepared jars with the vegetables and transfer the hot brine into the jars, leaving ½ inch headspace.
5. Rinse the rims of the jars with a dampened, clean, lint-free cloth or paper towel and again with a dry towel, then tighten the lids.
6. Transfer the covered jars to the water bath.
7. Finish the canning process in the water bath for 10 minutes.
8. Control the vacuum of the jars, turn them upside down and let cool them
9. Put the jars in the pantry and let flavor for about 2 weeks before consuming.

Nutrition:

Calories: 170

Carbs: 23g

Fat: 3g

Protein: 14g

80. Persimmon Butter

Preparation time: 15 minutes **Cooking time:** 15 minutes **Servings:** 5-6 pints   jar

Ingredients:

- 8 cups persimmon purée
- 1 cup orange juice
- 1 ½ cups honey
- grated zest of 1 orange

Directions:

1. Merge all the ingredients in a large stockpot; cook over medium-high heat until thick, about 10–15 minutes.
2. Ladle into sterilized jars, leaving ¼" headspace. Wipe rims; cap and seal. Process in water-bath canner 10 minutes.

Nutrition:

Calories: 14

Carbs: 4g

Fat: 0g

Protein: 0g

81. Canned Mushrooms

Preparation time: 15 minutes **Cooking time:** 25 minutes **Servings:** 10 pints jar

Ingredients:

- 7 lbs. tiny mushrooms, mixed, stems cut
- ½ cup lemon juice, bottled
- 2 quarts water
- 1 ½ cup olive oil
- 1 tbsp. dried oregano
- 1 tbsp. canning salt
- 12 garlic cloves, peeled
- 2 ½ cups white vinegar
- 1 tbsp. dried basil
- ½ cup onion, chopped fine
- 4 oz. pimientos, drained, chopped
- 25 peppercorns

Directions:

1. Sterilize the jars and distribute the garlic cloves and peppercorns in each. Combine the lemon juice and water in a pot and bring to boil.
2. Add in the mushrooms and leave to boil for 5 minutes. Drain and pack into the sterilized jars. Add the vinegar, oil, basil, salt, oregano, onions and pimientos in the pot and bring to boil again.
3. Pour the liquid into the sterilized jars, leaving half-inch of headspace and process for water bath canning for 20 minutes.

Nutrition:

Calories: 150

Fat: 15.3g

Carbohydrates: 3.3g

Proteins: 0.5g

82. Hot Green Beans

Preparation time: 15 minutes **Cooking time:** 10 minutes **Servings:** 4 pints jar

Ingredients:

- 2 lbs. green beans, tails and tops discarded
- 2 ½ cups water
- 2 hot chili peppers, halved
- ¼ cup caning salt
- 2 ½ cups cider vinegar
- 4 fresh dill heads
- 4 garlic cloves

Directions:

1. Sterilize the jars and set the garlic cloves, dill and hot peppers among each. Combine the salt, vinegar plus water in a pot and bring to boil. Pack the beans in the jars.
2. Spill the hot liquid into your sterilized jars, leaving quarter-inch of headspace and process for water canning and leave to process for 10 minutes.

Nutrition:

Calories: 14.4

Carbohydrates: 2.6g

Fat: 0g

Proteins: 0.6g

83. Canned Pumpkin

Preparation time: 15 minutes   **Cooking time:** 60 minutes   **Servings:** 12 pints jar

Ingredients:

- 256 oz. pumpkin, skin, seeds and gut discarded, chopped into cubes
- 1 tbsp. canning salt

Directions:

1. Sterilize the jars. Boil the pumpkin cubes for 2 minutes. Pack the pumpkin into the pints jar. Pour the hot juice that is released into the sterilized jars, leaving half-inch of headspace.
2. Secure the jars with the lid and apply the bands making sure that it is tightened.
3. Place in a boiling water canner and leave to process for 55 minutes. Detach, allow to cool, and then label the jars.

Nutrition:

Calories: 39

Carbohydrates: 9.2g

Fat: 0.3g

Proteins: 1.3g

84. Tomato Salsa

Preparation time: 15 minutes   **Cooking time:** 35 minutes   **Servings:** 7 pints jar

Ingredients:

- 2 cups tomato sauce
- 2 cups tomato paste
- 1 cup chopped green pepper
- 2 cups chopped onions
- 3-5 chopped jalapeno peppers, seeded
- 6 garlic cloves, minced
- ½ cup chopped fresh cilantro
- 2 tbsp. canning salt
- 2 tsp. ground cumin
- 2 tsp. pepper
- ⅔ cup white vinegar
- ⅓ cup sugar
- 5 lbs. chopped peeled tomatoes, drained

Directions:

1. In a stockpot, combine all ingredients. Bring to a boil. Reduce heat and let simmer within 20 minutes, uncovered, until vegetables are tender.
2. Scoop hot mixture into hot sterilized 1-pints jar, leaving ½ inch headspace. Detach air bubbles and if necessary, adjust headspace by adding hot mixture. Wipe the rims carefully. Set tops on jars and screw on bands until fingertip tight.
3. Set jars into canner with boiling water, ensuring that they are completely covered with water. Let boil for 15 minutes. Remove jars and cool.

Nutrition:

Calories: 24

Fat: 0g

Carbohydrates: 5g

Protein: 1g

85. Tomato Herb Jam

Preparation time: 15 minutes   **Cooking time:** 45 minutes   **Servings:** 4 pints jar

Ingredients:

- 6 lb. Plum tomatoes, cored and chopped
- 1 tsp. Salt
- ½ tsp. Black pepper, freshly grounded
- 3 Garlic cloves, chopped
- 2 Bay leaves
- 1 ½ cups Sugar
- 125ml Balsamic Vinegar
- 60ml Pinot Grigio

- 2 tsp. Herbes de Provence

Directions:

1. In a 6 Liter Stainless steel Dutch oven, mix cored and chopped plum tomatoes, salt, freshly grounded black pepper, chopped garlic cloves, and bay leaves.
2. Let it cook on medium-high flame and uncovered in the Dutch oven for about an hour or more with frequent stirring.
3. Now, add sugar and stir to dissolve it. Add balsamic vinegar, Pinot Grigio, and Herbes de Provence.
4. Simmer for about 45 minutes with continuous stirring until it becomes thick. Remove bay leaves and discard.
5. Transfer the hot jam into a hot jar with a ladle. Leave ¼ inch space on the top. Remove air bubbles. Clean the rim of the glass jar.
6. Place the lid and apply a band around it. Adjust to ensure that the lid is tight. Set the jar in the water bath canner that has boiling water. Leave the water bath canner for about 10 minutes.
7. Turn off the canner, remove the lid. Keep the jars in the canner for 5 minutes more. Remove the jars then allow them to cool. Store in the refrigerator.

Nutrition:

Calories: 20

Carbs: 4g

Fat: 0g

Protein: 0g

86. Peach Chili Tomato Sauce

Preparation time: 15 minutes   **Cooking time:** 20 minutes   **Servings:** 6 pints jar

Ingredients:

- 5 lbs. tomatoes
- 1½ lb. peaches, chopped
- 3 large sweet onions, chopped
- 3 medium pears, peeled, chopped
- 2 medium green peppers, chopped
- 2 jalapeno peppers, seeded, cut into matchsticks
- 2 celery ribs, chopped
- 1 tsp. mixed pickling spices
- 3 cups sugar
- 3 tsp. salt
- 2 cups white vinegar

Directions:

1. In a Dutch oven, bring 2 quarts water to a boil. Place 1-2 tomatoes in boiling water for 30-60. Remove and plunge into ice water. Peel and finely chop tomatoes.
2. Tie pickling spices in a cheesecloth bag. Place all ingredients in the pot. Bring to a boil.
3. Reduce heat and simmer, uncovered, 2-2½ hours until thickened, stirring occasionally. Discard spice bag.
4. Carefully scoop hot mixture into hot sterilized 1-pints jar, leaving ½-inch headspace.
5. Wipe the rims carefully. Set tops on jars and screw on bands until fingertip tight.
6. Set jars into canner with boiling water, ensuring that they are completely covered with water. Let boil for 20 minutes. Remove jars and cool.

Nutrition:

Calories: 40

Carbohydrates: 10g

Protein: 0g

Fats: 0g

87. Carrots and Jalapenos

Preparation time: 5 Minutes   **Cooking time:** 1 Hour and 20 Minutes   **Servings:** 4 pints jar

Ingredients:

- ½ cups vinegar, white and distilled
- ¼ cup sugar, white
- 10 Jalapeño peppers, sliced thinly
- 2 cups carrots, thinly sliced

- ½ red onion, sliced into thin rings

Directions:
1. Bring your sugar and vinegar in a large-sized saucepan. Bring this mixture to a boil over high heat. While cooking, make sure to stir thoroughly until your sugar fully dissolves.
2. Then add in your remaining ingredients. Stir to combine.
3. Detach from heat and let it stand for at least 1 hour.
4. Pour the mixture into your canning jars and seal with your lids.
5. Boil the jars in some boiling water for the next 10 minutes. Remove and let it cool slightly before placing it into your fridge. Use whenever you are ready.

Nutrition:

Calories: 104

Protein: 0g

Fiber: 0g

Fat: 1g

Carbs: 27g

88. Pepper Garlic Jelly

Preparation time: 5 Minutes   **Cooking time:** 30 Minutes   **Servings:** 4 pints jar

Ingredients:

- 2 cups peppers
- ½ cup Jalapeños
- 10 garlic cloves

- 2 cups vinegar
- 4 cups sugar
- 3 teaspoons pectin

Directions:
1. Combine peppers, garlic, and vinegar and bring to a boil.
2. Add sugar and pectin and boil until sugar dissolves.
3. Fill jars with the mixture.
4. Set in boiling water bath for 15 minutes.

Nutrition:

Calories: 393

Fat: 0.1g

Carbohydrates: 104.1g

Sugar: 99.8g

Protein: 0.4g

89. Roasted Red Pepper Jam

Preparation time: 15 Minutes   **Cooking time:** 1 ½ Hour   **Servings:** 6 pints jar

Ingredients:

- 6 pounds red bell peppers
- 1-pound tomatoes, plum, and Italian variety
- 2 garlic cloves, unpeeled
- 1 white onion, small and sliced thinly
- ½ cup vinegar, Red Wine variety

- 2 tablespoons basil, fresh and finely chopped
- 1 tablespoon sugar, white
- 1 teaspoon salt, to taste
- 5 canning jars, with lids and rings

Directions:
1. Roast your first 4 ingredients in your oven at 425 °F until your ingredients are soft and black on all sides. Once black, remove from the oven.
2. Allow your ingredients to cool completely before placing them into a food processor and blending on the highest setting until smooth consistency.
3. Place your mixture into a large-sized saucepan and add in your remaining ingredients. Stir until completely combined. Heat over medium heat and bring this mixture to a boil.
4. Once boiling, reduce the heat to low and simmer for the next 20 minutes. Detach from heat and allow to cool completely.

5. Pour the mixture into your canning jars and seal with your lids.
6. Boil the jars in some boiling water for the next 10 minutes. Remove and let it cool slightly before placing it into your fridge. Use whenever you are ready.

Nutrition:

Calories: 314

Fat: 0.2g

Protein: 0.9g

Sugar: 77.6g

Carbs: 81.1g

90. Spicy Style Tomato Jam

Preparation time: 5 Minutes

Cooking time: 1 Hour and 40 minutes

Servings: 4 pints jar

Ingredients:

- 3 lbs. tomatoes, fresh
- 1 gal. water, boiling
- 1 cup vinegar, Cider Variety
- ½ cup apple juice, fresh
- 1 ½ cup brown sugar, light and packed
- 1 ½ teaspoon salt, for taste
- ½ teaspoons black pepper, ground variety

- ½ teaspoons mustard, ground Variety
- ½ teaspoons allspice, ground Variety
- ½ teaspoons cumin, ground
- ¼ teaspoons of cayenne pepper
- 1 Lemon, cut into quarters, and sliced thinly

Directions:

1. Place your tomatoes into a large-sized pot. Pour in your boiling water and allow to sit for the next 5 minutes. After this time, remove your tomatoes and place them into a cold water bath until completely cool.
2. Then chop up your tomatoes in a food processor, making sure to reserve any juices.
3. Next, add your remaining ingredients except for your lemon and tomatoes into a large-sized saucepan and place over medium heat. Cook until your sugar fully dissolves.
4. Add in your chopped tomatoes and bring this mixture to a boil. Once boiling, reduce the heat to low and simmer for the next 30 to 45 minutes.
5. After this time, add in your lemon slices and continue to cook for the next 15 minutes.
6. After this time, remove from heat and set aside to cool completely.
7. Pour the mixture into your canning jars and seal with your lids.
8. Boil the jars in some boiling water for the next 10 minutes. Remove and let it cool slightly before placing it into your fridge. Use whenever you are ready.

Nutrition:

Carbohydrates: 3g

Sodium: 182mg

Fat: 0g

Calories: 14

Protein: 0g

91. Sweet Tasting Kiwi Jam

Preparation time: 15 Minutes

Cooking time: 12 Hours and 40 minutes

Servings: 10 pints jar

Ingredients:

- 24 kiwis, peeled and thoroughly mashed
- ¾ cup pineapple juice, fresh
- ¼ cup lemon juice, fresh

- 3 apples, unpeeled and cut into halves
- 4 cups sugar, white

Directions:

1. First, use a large-sized saucepan and bring your first 4 ingredients. Set over medium heat and bring this mixture to a boil.
2. Once boiling, add in your sugar and stir thoroughly to dissolve.

3. Then set the heat to low and continue to simmer for the next 30 minutes.
4. Pour the mixture into your canning jars and seal with your lids.
5. Boil the jars in some boiling water for the next 10 minutes. Remove and let it cool slightly before placing it into your fridge. Use whenever you are ready.

Nutrition:

Calories: 149   Carbs: 37.7g

Fat: 0.4g   Protein: 1.3g

92. Canned Asparagus

Preparation time: 5 Minutes   **Cooking time:** 30 Minutes   **Servings:** 4 pints jar

Ingredients:

- 20 asparagus
- 2 tablespoons salt
- 5 cups water
- 1 tablespoon chili flakes
- ¼ cup sugar

Directions:

1. Chop the asparagus finely and boil for 5 minutes.
2. Combine sugar, vinegar, salt, and water.
3. Boil until sugar dissolves.
4. Pack tightly into jars.
5. Pour sugar mixture into jars.
6. Set in boiling water canner for 10 minutes.

Nutrition:

Calories: 49   Protein: 3.6g

Fat: 0.2g   Sugars: 4.9g

Carbs: 8.7g

93. Tomato Juice

Preparation time: 15 minutes   **Cooking time:** 55 minutes   **Servings:** 10 pints jar

Ingredients:

- 14 lb. Tomatoes, cored and quartered
- 1 Large red beet, peeled and diced into cubes
- 1 tbsp. Salt
- ½ cup Lemon Juice, bottled

Directions:

1. Take a 6 Quarts or 6L Stainless Steel Stockpot or Dutch oven. Add tomatoes cored and diced into small pieces and allow them to boil. Stir occasionally.
2. Reduce the flame and let it simmer uncovered for about 15 minutes or more until it becomes soft.
3. Take a food mill and press the tomato mixture in different batches and transfer it into a large bowl. Discard tomato skin and seeds.
4. Transfer the tomato puree to the Dutch oven again and bring it to a boil at the medium flame with frequent stirring until the temperature reaches 88C°. Remove from the flame. Add lemon juice and stir well.
5. Transfer the hot tomato juice into a hot jar with a ladle. Leave 1-inch space on the top. Remove air bubbles. Clean the rim of the glass jar.
6. Set the lid and apply a band around it. Adjust to ensure that the lid is tight. Place the jar in the boiling water bath canner. Leave the water bath canner for about 40 minutes.
7. Turn off the canner, remove the lid. Keep the jars in the canner for 5 minutes more. Remove the jars then allow them to cool. Store in the refrigerator.

Nutrition:

Calories: 50   Carbs: 10g

Fat: 0g   Protein: 2g

94. Tomato Paste

Preparation time: 15 minutes   **Cooking time:** 0 minutes   **Servings:** 16 pints jar

Ingredients:

- 16 pounds Plum/Paste tomatoes, cubed
- 3 cups sweet pepper, chopped
- 2 Bay leaves
- 2 tbsp. Salt
- 3 Garlic cloves
- 6 tbsp. Lemon juice, bottled

Directions:

1. In a 6L Pot, mix all ingredients and cook on a medium flame for an hour with continuous stirring.
2. Remove bay leaves. Strain the mixture using a sieve. Return the mixture to your pot and cook for 3 hours over a medium-low flame with frequent stirring.
3. Transfer the hot jam into a hot jar with a ladle. Leave ½ inch space on the top. Remove air bubbles. Clean the rim of the glass jar.
4. Place the lid and apply a band around it. Adjust to ensure that the lid is tight. Place the jar in the water bath canner that has boiling water.
5. Leave the water bath canner for about 30 minutes. Turn off the canner, remove the lid. Keep the jars in the canner for 5 minutes more. Remove the jars then allow them to cool. Store in the refrigerator.

Nutrition:

Calories: 30   Fat: 0g

Carbs: 6g   Protein: 1g

95. Sundried Tomatoes

Preparation time: 5 Minutes   **Cooking time:** 8 to 12 Hours   **Servings:** 4 pints jar

Ingredients:

- 4 pounds fresh plum tomatoes (Italian Roma tomatoes), cut in two lengthwise
- 4 tablespoons dried basil
- 4 tablespoons Kosher salt
- 4 tablespoons brown sugar
- 4 tablespoons olive oil
- 2 garlic cloves, minced
- 1 tablespoon dried rosemary, or 2 fresh spring cut into 1inch pieces
- 4 garlic cloves, minced
- Olive oil to cover each jar

Directions:

1. Preheat the oven to 170 °F.
2. Add the basil, salt, sugar, olive oil, and garlic to a small mixing bowl. Combine well.
3. Place the tomatoes on a grill with a baking sheet underneath, cut side facing upward.
4. Sprinkle the spice mixture over the tomatoes.
5. Bake for 8 to 12 hours until the tomatoes are dried and shriveled up.
6. Remove from oven and let cool.
7. Distribute the tomatoes equally into each jar. Add the minced garlic and rosemary to each jar. Cover with olive oil.
8. Let all jars sit in a water bath for about 20 minutes.
9. Let cool completely before storing.

Nutrition:

Carbohydrates: 21g   Cholesterol: 0mg

Fat: 0g   Sugar: 0g

Protein: 0g

96. Black Beans and Corn Salsa

Preparation time: 5 Minutes   **Cooking time:** 60 Minutes   **Servings:** 4 pints jar

Ingredients:

- 2 cups frozen corn
- 15 oz. tomato sauce
- 12 oz. tomato paste
- ⅓ cup vinegar
- ⅛ cup salt
- 1 teaspoon black pepper

- 1 teaspoon cumin
- 6 garlic cloves, minced
- 1 Cubanelle pepper, chopped
- 1 cup Jalapeño pepper, chopped
- 1 ½ cups green peppers
- 2 ½ cups onion, chopped

Directions:

1. Into a large pot, mix everything, and bring to a slow boil for 10 minutes.
2. Then, ladle the salsa into jars.
3. Process for water bath canning for 10 minutes.

Nutrition:

Carbohydrates: 3g   Sodium: 182mg

Fat: 0g   Calories: 14

Protein: 0g

97. Carrot Pineapple and Pear Jam

Preparation time: 45 minutes   **Cooking time:** 5 minutes   **Servings:** 8 half-pints jar

Ingredients:

- 20 oz. crushed pineapple, undrained
- 1½ cups peeled, shredded carrots
- 1½ cups ripe, peeled, chopped pears
- 3 tbsp. lemon juice
- 1 tsp. ground cinnamon

- ¼ tsp. ground cloves
- ¼ tsp. ground nutmeg
- 1 package powdered fruit pectin
- 6½ cups erythritol

Directions:

1. In a saucepan over medium heat, merge first 7 ingredients and bring to a boil.
2. Set heat and simmer, covered, until pears are tender, 15-20 minutes, stirring occasionally.
3. Add pectin. Bring to a full boil, stirring constantly.
4. Stir in erythritol. Boil and stir for 1 minute.
5. Remove from heat and skim off foam.
6. Spoon the hot mixture in hot sterilized half-pints jar, leaving ¼-inch space of the top. Set jars into canner with boiling water, ensuring that they are completely covered with water. Let boil for 10 minutes. Remove jars and cool.

Nutrition:

Carbohydrates: 23g   Sodium: 2mg

Fat: 0g   Calories: 88

Protein: 0g

98. Radish Pickles

Preparation time: 10 minutes   **Cooking time:** 20 minutes   **Servings:** 4 pints jar

Ingredients:

- 2 pounds of radish (edges trimmed, sliced)
- 2 tablespoons of kosher salt
- 2 teaspoons of peppercorns
- 1 ¾ cup of white wine

- 10 cloves of garlic
- 3 tablespoons of sugar
- 1 cup of white wine vinegar
- 2 ½ cups of water
- ½ teaspoon of whole allspice

Directions:

1. Sterilize the jars. Mix the water and salt and add the sliced radish, chilling covered for 2 hours. Rinse and drain.
2. Pack the radish in the jars.
3. Merge the wine, peppercorns, vinegar, cloves, sugar, salt, and allspice in a saucepan. Set to a boil, reduce to low heat and cover for 15 minutes, stirring to dissolve the sugar.
4. Fill the sterilized jars halfway with the heated mixture, allowing a quarter-inch headspace.
5. Clean the rims and remove any air bubbles.
6. Place the lids on the jars and attach the bands, ensuring sure they are tight.
7. Set the jars for 10 minutes in a hot water canner that has been prepared. Remove the jars from the oven, let them cool, and then label them.

Nutrition:

Calories: 35

Total Fat: 0g

Total Carbohydrates: 4g

Proteins: 0g

99. Crisp Okra

Preparation time: 15 minutes   **Cooking time:** 45 minutes   **Servings:** 3 pints jar

Ingredients:

- 1 ½ lbs. fresh okra
- 3 dried red chili peppers
- 3 tsp. dried dill
- 2 cups water
- ½ cup apple cider vinegar
- ½ cup white vinegar
- 2 tbsp. salt

Directions:

1. Wash and rinse your okra thoroughly before placing them in your sterilized jars.
2. Place an equal amount of okra, chili, and dill in each of the jars.
3. Combine the salt, vinegar, and water in a small saucepan and bring it to a boil.
4. Set the hot liquid into each jar, leaving a good headspace.
5. Prepare the jars for proper sealing according to the processing Instructions.
6. Have your water canner ready and filled halfway with water. Allow water to boil before placing the jars on the rack. Be sure to leave enough space around the jars and enough water to cover them. Set the water to a rolling boil, cover, and start the 10 minutes processing time.

Nutrition:

Calories: 352

Fat: 0.2g

Carbohydrates: 92g

Sugar: 90g

Protein: 0.5g

100.   Sliced Red Onions

Preparation time: 30 minutes   **Cooking time:** 10 minutes   **Servings:** 3 pints jar

Ingredients:

- 1 cup water
- 1 cup white/apple cider vinegar
- ⅓ cup sugar
- 5 ¼ tbsp. pickling salt
- 2 lbs. red onions
- 1 ½ tsp. peppercorns
- 3 bay leaves

Directions:

1. Peel and slice your onions thinly. Sprinkle on 1 ¾ tsp pickling salt and toss to combine. Let them rest for 30 minutes before rinsing them.
2. In your prepared jars, divide the bay leaves and peppercorn equally. Then, pack the sliced onions in each jar by pressing them down, but ensure they're loosely packed.

3. Set the brine by combining the rest of the ingredients in a pot on low heat. Bring to a simmer while continuously stirring until all the granules have dissolved.
4. Pour the brine over the contents in your jars, leaving an appropriate headspace. Prepare the jars for closing as instructed.
5. Get your water bath ready and bring to a boil. Gently place the jars in while allowing it to boil again. Cover with the lid and wait for the processing time of 10 minutes.

Nutrition:

Calories: 202

Fat: 0g

Carbohydrates: 53g

Sugar: 53g

Protein: 0.2g

Chapter 7.   Salsa and Sauces

101.   Tangy Cranberry Sauce

Preparation time: 10 minutes   **Cooking time:** 15 minutes   **Servings:** 5 pints jar

Ingredients:

- 4 (12-ounces) bags fresh cranberries (8 cups)
- 2 cups sugar
- 2 cups water
- 2 cups bottled orange juice
- 2 large oranges, peeled, pith removed, seeded, and chopped
- ½ teaspoon ground allspice (optional)
- ½ teaspoon ground cloves (optional)

Directions:

1. In a smaller pot, attach lids and rings, 1 tbsp. distilled white vinegar, and water to cover. Boil for 5 minutes, then detach from heat.
2. In a large pot, combine the cranberries, sugar, water, orange juice, oranges, allspice, and cloves. Set to a boil over medium-high heat, stirring often. Set the heat to low and simmer for 15 minutes. Stir often, muddling the orange pieces with your spoon. Remove from heat.
3. Set the hot jars on a cutting board. Using a funnel, ladle the hot sauce into the jars, leaving a ½ inch headspace. Detach any air bubbles and add additional sauce if necessary to maintain the ½ inch headspace.
4. Clean the jar with a warm washcloth dipped in distilled white vinegar. Set a lid and ring on each jar and hand-tighten.
5. Bring the jars in the water bather, ensuring each jar is covered by at least 1 inch of water. Attach 2 tablespoons distilled white vinegar to the water and turn the heat to high. Set the canner to a boil and process both quarts and pints for 15 minutes. When processed, wait 5 minutes before removing the jars from the canner.

Nutrition:

Calories: 25   Carbs: 6g

Fat: 0g   Protein: 0g

102.   Spaghetti Sauce with Tomato

Preparation time: 20 minutes   **Cooking time:** 2-3 hours minutes   **Servings:** 20 pints jar

Ingredients:

- 30 to 35 pounds (14-16 kg) fresh canning tomatoes
- 1 tablespoon olive oil
- 1 medium onion, finely chopped
- 2 cloves garlic, minced
- 2 bay leaves
- 2 tablespoons garlic powder
- 1 teaspoon parsley flakes
- 1 teaspoon Italian seasoning
- 1 teaspoon dried oregano
- 1 teaspoon dried basil
- 1 teaspoon dried summer savory
- 1 teaspoon dried tarragon
- 1 teaspoon white pepper
- 1 tablespoon salt
- 1 teaspoon onion powder
- 2 tablespoons organic or non-GMO granulated sugar
- 2 tablespoons lemon juice per jar

Directions:

1. Wash tomatoes and cut off any bruised or damaged areas. Blanch the tomatoes. This process is easily done in stages and requires a large pot of boiling water and another pot or bowl of ice water. Set a pot of water to a boil and add in tomatoes once the pot begins to boil. Set the timer for 1 minute.

Use a slotted spoon to carefully detach the tomatoes from the hot water and put them in the ice bath. You should see the tomato skins split while in the boiling water or once added to the ice bath. Redo this process until all the tomatoes are blanched. This method will make removing the skins from the tomatoes a quick job, as the skin will easily fall off the fruit with a little rub of the fingers. Then, core the tomatoes and cut them into quarters.

2. Once all tomatoes are blanched, peeled, cored, and cut, add them to a large (at least 7 quarts) pot. Using a hand blender, break down the tomatoes into the consistency you want your sauce to have.

3. In a medium frying pan, warmth the olive oil and sauté the onion and garlic. Once the onion is translucent, it's done; this typically takes about 5 minutes. Add mixture to the tomatoes and add in all the seasonings. Mix well and heat the pot to a medium-high simmer. The sauce will need to cook for 2 to 3 hours to thicken. It must be stirred occasionally to avoid burning.

4. Once the sauce has thickened, detach the bay leaves. Prepare the quart jars with 2 tablespoons of lemon juice per jar. This will add acidity to the sauce that will keep it from growing unsafe bacteria.

5. Ladle the sauce into warm, prepared jars. Use a funnel to safely transfer the sauce, leaving ½ inch of headspace. Clean the jars with a dampened, clean, lint-free cloth or paper towel and again with a dry towel. Place canning lid on the jar and twist the canning ring on until it's just-snug on the jar. Set the jars into the canning pot, and make sure the jars are covered by at least 1 inch of water. Set the lid on the canning pot and once the water bath reaches a rolling boil, set the timer and process in the water bath for 40 minutes. Carefully remove jars from the water bath with canning tongs and place the jars on a towel-lined surface for 12 to 24 hours without touching.

Nutrition:

Calories: 314

Protein: 0.9g

Carbs: 81.1g

Fat: 0.2g

Sugar: 77.6g

103.   Tomato Ketchup with Vinegar

Preparation time: 25 minutes   **Cooking time:** 45 minutes   **Servings:** 6 pints jar

Ingredients:

- 7 pounds (3.2 kg) Roma or other paste tomatoes
- 1 large onion, chopped
- 1 cup apple cider vinegar
- ½ cup firmly packed brown sugar
- 2 teaspoons kosher salt
- ¼ teaspoon cayenne pepper
- 1 teaspoon mustard seed
- 1 teaspoon whole cloves
- 1 teaspoon whole allspice berries
- 1 cinnamon stick, broken

Directions:

1. In a large pot, merge the tomatoes and onion. Bring the mixture to a boil. Reduce the heat to low. Parboil for 30 minutes, or until very soft.

2. Using a food mill, pass the mixture through to purée. Discard the seeds and skins. Rinse the pot, place it on the stove, and return the purée to it.

3. Prepare a hot water bath. Set the jars in it to keep warm. Clean the lids and rings in hot, soapy water, and set aside.

4. Add the cider vinegar, brown sugar, kosher salt, and cayenne pepper to the purée.

5. In a cheesecloth square, combine the mustard seed, cloves, allspice, and cinnamon. Tie securely with kitchen twine into a sachet. Add to the pot. Simmer over low heat for about 1 hour, 30 minutes, or until reduced by half. Remove and discard the sachet.

6. Ladle the hot ketchup into the prepared jars, leaving ½ inch of headspace. Clean the rims clean and seal with the lids and rings.

7. Set the jars in a hot water bath for 10 minutes. Se off the heat and let the jars rest in the water bath for 10 minutes.

8. Carefully detach the jars from the hot water canner. Set aside to cool for 12 hours.

9. Check the lids for proper seals. Detach the rings, wipe the jars, label and date them, and set to a cupboard or pantry.
10. Use within 4 weeks.

Nutrition:

Calories: 37

Protein: 1.9g

Carbs: 7.4g

Fat: 0.8g

Sugar: 1.3g

104.   Lime Blueberry Ketchup

Preparation time: 5 minutes   **Cooking time:** 15 minutes   **Servings:** 3 pints jar

Ingredients:

- 2 cups fresh or frozen blueberries
- ⅓ cup apple cider vinegar
- 2 tablespoons balsamic vinegar
- Juice of 1 lime
- ¾ cup firmly packed brown sugar

- 1 teaspoon ground cinnamon
- ½ teaspoon ground cloves
- ½ teaspoon ground ginger
- ½ teaspoon salt
- ¼ teaspoon cayenne pepper

Directions:

1. Prepare a hot water bath. Set the jars in it to keep warm. Wash the lids and rings and set aside.
2. In a medium saucepan, merge the blueberries, cider vinegar, balsamic vinegar, and lime juice. Bring to a boil. Reduce the heat to medium. Simmer for 5 minutes. Set the blueberry mixture through a sieve into a clean saucepan, pressing with a rubber spatula or wooden spoon to extract as much pulp as possible. Discard the seeds.
3. Add the brown sugar, cinnamon, cloves, ginger, salt, and cayenne pepper to the blueberry mixture. Set to a full rolling boil over high heat, stirring to dissolve the sugar. Reduce the heat to medium. Parboil for about 10 minutes more, or until thickened.
4. Ladle the hot blueberry ketchup into the prepared jars, leaving ¼ inch of headspace. Use a nonmetallic utensil to free any air bubbles. Clean the rims clean and seal with the lids and rings.
5. Set the jars in a hot water bath for 15 minutes. Set off the heat and let the jars rest in the water bath for 10 minutes.
6. Carefully detach the jars from the hot water canner. Set aside to cool.
7. Detach the rings, wipe the jars, label and date them, and transfer to a cupboard or pantry.
8. Refrigerate and use within 3 weeks. Properly secure jars will last in the cupboard for 12 months.

Nutrition:

Calories: 22

Total fat: 0.2g

Carbs: 3g

Protein: 2.8g

Sugars: 1g

Fiber: 1g

105.   Classic Fiesta Salsa

Preparation time: 15 Minutes   **Cooking time:** 2 hours   **Servings:** 3 pints jar

Ingredients:

- 4 ½ cups tomatoes, fresh and finely diced
- 3 tablespoons vinegar, white

- ¼ cup salsa, your favorite kind
- 2, 16 oz. canning jars, with lids and rings

Directions:

1. Combine your diced tomatoes, vinegar, and favorite salsa in a large-sized saucepan placed over medium heat.
2. Cook the mixture until boiling. After your mixture is boiling, reduce the heat to low then simmer for the next 5 minutes.
3. Detach from heat and let it cool slightly.
4. Pour the mixture into your canning jars and seal with your lids.

5. Boil the jars in some boiling water for the next 10 minutes. Remove and let it cool slightly before placing it into your fridge. Use whenever you are ready.

Nutrition:

Calories: 302

Fat: 0.1g

Carbohydrates: 79.8g

Sugar: 77.7g

Protein: 0.6g

---

106.   Chipotle Style Plum Sauce

Preparation time: 5 Minutes

Cooking time: 4 Hours and 40 Minutes

Servings: 8 half-pints jar

Ingredients:

- 5 quarts plums, ripped and pitted
- 4 garlic cloves, pressed
- 1 onion, finely diced
- 6 cups sugar, white
- ½ cup vinegar, apple cider variety
- 2 tablespoons chipotle seasoning, Southwest Variety
- 1 tablespoon garlic seasoning, Roasted Variety
- 1 Jalapeño pepper, finely diced
- 7 teaspoons salt, for taste
- 1 teaspoon Smoke Flavoring, liquid variety
- 8 canning jars, with lids and rings

Directions:

1. First, place your plums into a colander set inside a large-sized bowl and squeeze to force the juices out. Repeat until all your plums have been juiced.
2. Pour this juice along with your garlic and onion into a medium-sized saucepan and place over medium heat. Set this mixture to a boil before reducing the heat to low. Continue to simmer until your onions turn translucent.
3. Then pour this mixture into a large-sized pot and add in your remaining ingredients. Stir thoroughly until your salt and sugar fully dissolve. Set this mixture to a boil over medium heat. Once boiling, reduce the heat to low and cook until your mixture is thick inconsistency. This should take about 1 ½ hours.
4. After this time, detach from heat and let it cool completely.
5. Pour the mixture into your canning jars and seal with your lids.
6. Boil the jars in some boiling water for the next 10 minutes. Remove and let it cool slightly before placing it into your fridge. Use whenever you are ready.

Nutrition:

Calories: 393

Fat: 0.1g

Carbohydrates: 104.1g

Sugar: 99.8g

Protein: 0.4g

Cholesterol: 0mg

---

107.   Harvest Time Tomato Marinara Sauce

Preparation time: 15 Minutes

Cooking time: 5 hours

Servings: 20 pints jar

Ingredients:

- 25 lbs. tomatoes, plum variety, cored and cut in halves
- 3 bay leaves, fresh
- 1 ½ tablespoon honey, raw
- 1 tablespoon oregano, dried
- 1 tablespoon salt, to taste
- 2 teaspoons ground black pepper
- ½ cup olive oil, extra virgin
- 1 lb. onions, yellow in color, and finely chopped
- 10 garlic cloves, minced
- 10, 1 quart canning jars, with lids and rings
- 10 teaspoons salt, to taste and evenly divided
- 1 ¾ cups lemon juice, fresh and evenly divided

Directions:

1. First, place your first 6 ingredients into a large-sized saucepan. Cover with some water and stir thoroughly to combine.
2. Secure and bring this mixture to a boil over medium to high heat.
3. Once boiling, reduce the heat to low and simmer for the next 20 minutes uncovered, making sure to stir thoroughly. After this time, remove your bay leaves and season to your taste.
4. Next, heat your olive oil in a large-sized skillet placed over medium to high heat. Once your oil is hot enough, add in your onions and garlic and cook until your onions are soft to the touch. This should take about 10 minutes.
5. Next, puree your tomatoes until smooth in consistency and add back to your saucepan. Add in your cooked garlic and onions and cook while uncovered over medium to high heat until your sauce becomes a thick consistency. This should take about 1 to 1 ½ hour.
6. Remove from heat and let it cool slightly.
7. Pour the mixture into your canning jars and seal with your lids.
8. Boil the jars in some boiling water for the next 10 minutes. Remove and let it cool slightly before placing it into your fridge. Use whenever you are ready.

Nutrition:

Calories: 159   Sugar: 4.4g

Fat: 12.7g   Protein: 0.8g

Carbohydrates: 8.6g

---

108.   Carolina Style BBQ Peppers

Preparation time: 5 Minutes   **Cooking time:** 20 Minutes   **Servings:** 6 pints jar

Ingredients:

- 2 cups oil, corn variety
- 2 cups vinegar, cider variety
- 2 cups sugar, white
- 4 cups Ketchup, your favorite kind
- 1 lb. Jalapeño peppers, fresh and sliced into thin rings
- Dash oregano, dried
- 1 garlic clove, minced

Directions:

1. First, use a large-sized pot, add in your first 4 ingredients, and stir thoroughly until your sugar is fully dissolved.
2. Bring this mixture to a boil. Once boiling, add in your jalapeno peppers. Stir to combine.
3. Set your heat to low and allow your mixture to simmer for the next 10 minutes before seasoning with a dash of garlic and oregano. Remove from heat and let it cool completely.
4. Pour the mixture into your canning jars and seal with your lids.
5. Boil the jars in some boiling water for the next 10 minutes. Remove and let it cool slightly before placing it into your fridge. Use whenever you are ready.

Nutrition:

Calories: 396   Sugar: 102g

Fat: 0.1g   Protein: 0.3g

Carbohydrates: 104g

---

109.   Thai Dipping Sauce

Preparation time: 5 Minutes   **Cooking time:** 40 Minutes   **Servings:** 4 pints jar

Ingredients:

- 4 cups vinegar
- 4 cups sugar
- ½ cup red pepper flakes
- 1 tablespoon salt

Directions:

1. Heat vinegar. Add sugar to it and boil until it dissolves.

2. Add garlic, pepper flakes, salt.
3. Boil for 2 minutes.
4. Ladle into your prepared jars and process in boiling water canner for 15 minutes.

Nutrition:

Calories: 50   Fat: 0g

Carbs: 10g   Protein: 2g

---

110.   Barbecue Sauce

Preparation time: 15 Minutes   **Cooking time:** 2 Hours   **Servings:** 4 pints jar

Ingredients:

- 3 onions
- 5 garlic cloves
- 1 tablespoon oil
- 6 cups tomato sauce
- 1 ½ cups vinegar
- 4 tablespoons chili powder
- 2 teaspoons paprika
- ½ cup honey
- Salt

Directions:

1. Sauté the onions and garlic in oil.
2. Attach all the other ingredients and bring to a boil.
3. Simmer for 45 minutes.
4. Transfer into jars.
5. Process in your boiling water canner for 20 minutes.

Nutrition:

Calories: 150   Carbohydrates: 3.3g

Fat: 15.3g   Proteins: 0.5g

---

111.   Zesty Salsa

Preparation time: 5 Minutes   **Cooking time:** 10 Minutes   **Servings:** 6 pints jar

Ingredients:

- 10 cups chopped tomatoes
- 5 cups chopped and seeded bell peppers
- 5 cups chopped onions
- 2 ½ cups hot peppers, chopped and seeded
- 1 ¼ cup cider vinegar
- 3 minced garlic cloves
- 2 tablespoons cilantro, minced
- 3 teaspoons salt
- 1 can tomato paste, about six ounces

Directions:

1. Put all the ingredients except for the tomato paste into a large pot.
2. Let simmer for about three minutes or until thick.
3. Mix in the tomato paste.
4. Ladle the hot salsa into jars, leaving about ¼ inch headspace.
5. Let all jars sit in a water bath for about 20 minutes.
6. Allow to cool completely before storing.

Nutrition:

Carbohydrates: 1g   Sodium: 727mg

Fat: 0g   Calories: 4g

Protein: 1g

---

112.   Homemade Pizza Sauce

Preparation time: 15 Minutes   **Cooking time:** 80 Minutes   **Servings:** 10 pints jar

Ingredients:

- 25-28 red and ripe tomatoes, medium-sized
- 2 large yellow onions, peeled
- 4 large garlic cloves, peeled
- 3 tablespoons olive oil
- 2 tablespoons lemon juice
- 1 teaspoon freshly ground black pepper

- 1 tablespoon white sugar
- 2 tablespoons parsley, chopped
- 1 tablespoon oregano
- 1 tablespoon dry basil
- 1 teaspoon dry rosemary
- 1 teaspoon celery seed
- 2 teaspoons kosher salt

Directions:
1. Peel the tomatoes. Set them for two to three minutes in boiling water so they are easier to peel. Set them in a blender or food processor.
2. Mince the onions and garlic cloves.
3. Sauté the onions and garlic in a large saucepan with olive oil for about 34 minutes until tender and fragrant.
4. Add the tomato puree. Bring to a boil on medium-high heat. Lower the heat and let it parboil for 45 minutes.
5. Once the sauce thickens, put it into jars.
6. Allow your jars to sit in a water bath for 25 minutes.
7. Let cool completely before storing.

Nutrition:

Calories: 170

Fat: 3g

Carbs: 23g

Protein: 14g

113.   Unripe Tomato Salsa

Preparation time: 5 Minutes   **Cooking time:** 60 Minutes   **Servings:** 8 pints jar

Ingredients:

- 5 lbs. unpeeled green tomatoes, finely chopped
- 6 yellow onions, chopped small
- 3 Jalapeños, chopped with the seeds
- 4 large green bell peppers, chopped
- 6 garlic cloves, minced

- 1 cup fresh cilantro, chopped
- 1 cup lime juice
- 1 tablespoon salt
- ½ tablespoon cumin
- 1 tablespoon dried oregano leaves
- 2 tablespoons pepper

Directions:
1. Merge all your ingredients in a large pot and bring to a boil, mixing for the next 30 to 40 minutes.
2. After the time is up and it's at a boil again, put the salsa into the sterilized jars. Allow the jars to sit in a water bath for 15 to 20 minutes.

Nutrition:

Calories: 302

Sugar: 77.7g

Fat: 0.1g

Protein: 0.6g

Carbohydrates: 79.8g

114.   Applesauce

Preparation time: 15 Minutes   **Cooking time:** 20 Minutes   **Servings:** 3 pints jar

Ingredients:

- 3 lbs. cooking apples such as McIntosh, Cortland, or Bramley
- 2 tablespoons white sugar (optional)

- 2 teaspoons ground cinnamon (optional)
- Water

Directions:
1. Peel, core, and then quarter the apples, put into a large pot, cook until soft.

2. Puree the apples, and then put the mixture back into the pan and bring to a boil. Add sugar or cinnamon if desired.
3. Place into jars while boiling.
4. Let your jars sit in a water bath for about 20 minutes.
5. Let cool completely before storing.

Nutrition:

Calories: 20

Carbs: 4g

Fat: 0g

Protein: 0g

---

115. Asian Plum Sauce

Preparation time: 5 Minutes   **Cooking time:** 60 Minutes   **Servings:** 4 pints jar

Ingredients:

- 4 garlic cloves, minced
- ¼ cup fresh ginger, grated
- 1 yellow onion, diced finely
- 1 cup brown sugar
- 2 cups water
- ⅛ cup Teriyaki sauce
- 1 teaspoon sesame oil
- ⅛ cup soy sauce
- ½ teaspoon crushed and dried chili
- 3 lbs. chopped and pitted plums
- 1 tablespoon cornstarch
- 1 lemon, squeezed for the juice

Directions:

1. Mix all ingredients, then bring to a boil in a large pot for about 30 minutes.
2. Simmer for around 58 minutes or until it is thick, and then put into jars.
3. Let your jars sit in a water bath for about 10 minutes.
4. Let cool completely before storing. Store in a cool and dark place.

Nutrition:

Calories: 37

Protein: 1.9g

Carbs: 7.4g

Fat: 0.8g

---

116. Pear Sauce

Preparation time: 2 hours 45 minutes   **Cooking time:** 20 minutes

Servings: 5 pints jar

Ingredients:

- 14-16 pears (if using small pears, you may want to include up to 20)
- Cinnamon to taste (about ½ teaspoon per jar); this is an optional ingredient

Directions:

1. To prepare the pear sauce, you'll need large spoons and ladles, jar lifters, and a water bath canner. Pears should be scrubbed and washed thoroughly with a scrub and cold water. Remove any labels, stickers, and then peel using a paring knife or peeler. This process is optional, and you may decide to leave the peel intact, as it can be removed later with a sieve, along with the stems and seeds.
2. Chop the pears with a knife by hand or use a core-cutting device that simultaneously slices the pears into pieces while taking out the seeds inside. A food mill can also remove the seeds so that you do not have to peel manually.
3. Place the pears in a large cooking pot and cover with water, then cover and heat on high, bringing the contents to a boil. Once the boiling point is reached, reduce the heat to medium-high and continue to cook for another 10-15 minutes or until the pears are tender. They should be mushy enough to mash through a sieve and remove any excess seeds, peeling, and stems not removed prior to this step. Push the pears through a sieve and into a large bowl that's sterilized.
4. Set the jars by washing them in warm water and soap, then set them in boiling water for at least 10 minutes, along with the lids. Use a jar lifter to remove them and place on a cloth, then gently scoop

the pear sauce in each jar, leaving ½ inch at the top. Fasten the lids on each jar and prepare the water bath.

5. Add the filled jars into a water bath canner and cover with water to one inch above each. Bring to a boil and cover, then process for about 10-12 minutes. Remove with a jar lifter and set on a wire rack or cloth on the countertop. Leave the pear sauce overnight to cool, then store in a pantry or cold, dark area for up to one year.

Nutrition:

Calories: 79

Carbs: 21g

Fat: 0g

Protein: 0g

117.   Apple Sauce

Preparation time: 45 minutes   **Cooking time:** 20 minutes   **Servings:** 4 pints jar

Ingredients:

- Apples (about 20 in total, or three pounds)
- Water
- Lemon juice, bottled (optional)
- Sugar (optional)
- Cinnamon (optional)

Directions:

1. Pour water and lemon juice into a large cooking pot. The amount of water should cover about ⅓ of the interior. Ascorbic acid can be used in place of lemon juice, if available, or this ingredient can be omitted altogether. Peel, core, and slice the apples, removing all the seeds. As each apple is peeled, set inside the water so that it does not brown. Rinse each apple before adding to the cooking pot. Add any sugar and cinnamon as desired, or wait to add these ingredients later, if you're uncertain at this point.

2. Bring the apples to a boil, and stir regularly, then reduce the heat to a simmer and cook for five minutes for about 30 minutes, or until all the apples are tender or soft. Some apples, depending on the variety, can soften while others need more time. Once they soften, apples will be easy to break down in a food mill or sieve, then set in a blender or food processor. If you prefer a chunky texture, skip the blender and mash lightly until you achieve the desired consistency.

3. Set the sauce to the pot and add the sugar and cinnamon, then cook and bring back to a boil. Transfer the apple sauce into sterilized jars and add a bit of lemon juice, if desired. Give ½ inch of space at the top of each jar. Wipe the rims of each jar and place the lids on tightly. Set the jars in the water bath canner or a pressure canner for about 8-10 minutes, then detach from heat and allow to cool on a wire rack or cloth on the countertop. Set the jars in cool place or the pantry for up to one year.

Nutrition:

Calories: 36.4

Sugars: 1g

Total fat: 0.13g

Fiber: 2.34g

Carbs: 8.36g

Sodium: 87.1mg

Protein: 1.17g

118.   Mango Salsa

Preparation time: 45 minutes   **Cooking time:** 20 minutes   **Servings:** 3 pints jar

Ingredients:

- 6 cups of mangoes, diced thinly
- Brown sugar, 1 cup
- Garlic cloves, 2
- ½ cup of water
- Medium red onion, finely diced
- Red bell pepper, sliced finely and seeds removed about 1 ½ cups
- Red pepper flakes, ½ teaspoon
- Fresh cilantro, two teaspoons
- Chopped fresh ginger, two teaspoons

- Vinegar (white or cider), about one ¼ cups

Directions:

1. In a large cooking pot, toss in the ingredients and bring them to a boil over a high temperature. Stir regularly until the sugar dissolves. Set the temperature in low to a simmer and continue cooking for about five minutes. Scoop the mixture with a slotted spoon and transfer into all the jars, leaving about ½ inch at the top of each. Add a bit of liquid to the top, not including the ½ inch of space. If there isn't enough room at the top, reduce slightly with a smaller spoon until this is achieved.
2. Wipe the rim and outside of the jars with a clean towel with a small amount of vinegar. Affix the lids and process the jars in boiling water (water bath canner) for about 15-17 minutes. If the size of the jars is smaller, such as a half pint, then process for about 10 minutes.

Nutrition:

Calories: 49

Fat: 0.2g

Carbs: 8.7g

Protein: 3.6g

Sugars: 4.9g

119. Mexican-Inspired Salsa

Preparation time: 10 minutes   **Cooking time:** 30 minutes   **Servings:** 6 pints jar

Ingredients:

- 8 large cloves garlic, chopped
- 4 medium jalapeños, chopped
- 2 ½ cups diced onion
- 2 ½ cups diced green bell peppers
- 9 cups chopped tomatoes
- 1 ½ cup tomato paste
- 1 cup white vinegar
- 6 teaspoons canning salt

Directions:

1. Boil the whole tomatoes in water for at least 1 minutes; remove and let cool. Peel to remove the skin and then add to a pot along with the remaining ingredients.
2. Simmer for about 30 minutes. transfer the salsa to sterile jars and seal. Bring in a hot water bath for about 30 minutes. let cool and store in the fridge.

Nutrition:

Calories: 26

Total Fat: 0.2g

Carbs: 5.2g

Sugars: 3.4g

Protein: 1.1g

120. Delicious Red Onion and Tomato Salsa

Preparation time: 30 minutes   **Cooking time:** 1 hour 20 minutes   **Servings:** 8 pints jar

Ingredients:

- 3 red onions, chopped
- 4 green peppers, chopped
- 10 pounds tomatoes, quartered
- 3 cups tomato paste
- 1 ¾ cups white vinegar
- ½ teaspoon hot pepper sauce
- ¼ cup canning salt
- 5 jalapeno peppers, seeded and chopped
- 15 garlic cloves, minced
- 1 celery rib, chopped
- 1 medium sweet red pepper, chopped
- ½ cup sugar

Directions:

1. In a pot, boil tomatoes for about 20 minutes or until tender; drain and reserve the cooking liquid.
2. Return to the pot and add in remaining ingredients; cook for about 1 hour and then remove from heat. Transfer to sterile jars and seal. Bring in a hot water bath for about 30 minutes and then let cool before storing in the fridge or freezer.

Nutrition:

Calories: 14

Total Fat: 0g

Carbs: 3g

Sugars: 2g

Protein: 0g

Cholesterol: 0mg

Sodium: 182mg

121.   Salsa Verde

Preparation time: 15 Minutes   **Cooking time:** 10 Minutes   **Servings:** 4 pints jar

Ingredients:

- 12 medium green tomatoes, cored, peeled, and diced
- 6 to 8 Jalapeños, seeded and minced
- 2 large red onions, diced
- 1 teaspoon minced garlic

- ½ cup fresh lime juice
- ½ cup fresh chopped cilantro
- 1 ½ teaspoon ground cumin
- 1 teaspoon dried oregano
- Salt and pepper, to taste

Directions:

1. Prepare your water bath canner, your lids and bands.
2. Combine all tomatoes, jalapenos, onion, garlic, and lime juice in a large saucepan.
3. Cover and bring to a boil, then stir in the remaining ingredients.
4. Reduce heat and simmer for 5 minutes, then spoon this mixture into the jars, leaving about ½ inch of headspace.
5. Clean the rims, add the lid, seal with a metal band, place your jars in your water bath canner, and set the water to boil.
6. Process the jars for about 20 minutes, then remove the jars and wipe them dry.
7. Place all jars on your canning rack and cool for at least 24 hours before storing them.

Nutrition:

Calories: 50

Carbs: 2g

Fat: 0g

Protein: 10g

122.   Fresh Green Salsa

Preparation time: 10 minutes   **Cooking time:** 30 minutes   **Servings:** 8 pints jar

Ingredients:

- 2 jalapeno peppers, diced
- 6 green onions, sliced
- 7 cups tomatoes, diced
- 4 cloves garlic, minced
- 2 tablespoons minced cilantro

- 4 drops hot pepper sauce
- 2 tablespoons lime juice
- ½ cup vinegar
- 2 teaspoons salt

Directions:

1. Merge all ingredients in a pan; set to a boil and then simmer for about 15 minutes. ladle in sterile jars and seal. Bring in a hot water bath for about 15 minutes and then let cool before storing in the fridge.

Nutrition:

Calories: 5

Total Fat: 0g

Carbs: 0.4g

Sugars: 0.6g

Protein: 0.2g

123.   Simple Salsa

Preparation time: 5 Minutes   **Cooking time:** 10 Minutes   **Servings:** 4 pints jar

Ingredients:

- 5 cups slicing tomatoes (peeled, cored, and chopped)
- 2 cups green chilies (seeded and chopped)
- 1 cup onions (chopped in fine bites)
- ½ cup Jalapeño peppers (seeded and chopped)
- 4 garlic cloves (chopped finely)
- 1 teaspoon ground cumin
- 1 tablespoon cilantro
- 1 tablespoon oregano
- 2 cups distilled white vinegar
- 1 ½ teaspoon table salt

Directions:
1. Merge all the ingredients in a large pot. Place the pot on the stove and bring to a rolling boil while constantly stirring to prevent burning.
2. Set the heat a little bit and allow the mixture to simmer for 20 minutes. Stir frequently.
3. Divide the salsa among 4 jars. Make sure to leave about ½ inch of space at the top of each jar. Place the lids on your jars and process using the water bath canning Direction for 15 to 25 minutes.

Nutrition:

Carbohydrates: 23g

Fat: 0g

Protein: 0g

Sodium: 2mg

Calories: 88

---

124.   Mango Pineapple Salsa

Preparation time: 15 Minutes   **Cooking time:** 2 Hours   **Servings:** 5 pints jar

Ingredients:

- ½ teaspoon salt
- 2 garlic cloves, minced
- 1 teaspoon fresh ginger, grated
- ¼ cup cider vinegar
- ¼ lime juice
- ⅓ cup sugar
- ¼ cup Jalapeños, finely chopped
- 1 cup red sweet pepper
- 1 cup large sweet onion
- 2 cups mangoes, peeled, chopped
- 3 cups pineapple
- 4 cups ripe tomatoes, cored, chopped

Directions:
1. Combine all ingredients in a large pot. Bring to an uncovered for 10 minutes. Stirring occasionally. Then, remove from heat.
2. Ladle salsa into jars with ½ inch headspace.
3. Process all jars in boiling water for 20 minutes. Then, remove jars and let cool for 12 hours.

Nutrition:

Calories: 314

Protein: 0.9g

Carbs: 81.1g

Fat: 0.2g

Sugar: 77.6g

---

125.   Red Tomato Ketchup

Preparation time: 15 Minutes   **Cooking time:** 80 minutes   **Servings:** 16 pints jar

Ingredients:

- 3 tablespoons celery seeds
- 4 teaspoons whole cloves
- 2 cinnamon sticks
- 1 ½ teaspoon whole allspice
- 3 cups cider vinegar
- 24 lbs. red tomatoes, cored and quartered
- 3 cups chopped onions
- 1 teaspoon cayenne pepper
- 1 ½ cups granulated sugar
- ½ cup pickling salt such as Ball salt, and preserving salt

Directions:
1. Create a spice bag with the first 4 ingredients by wrapping them in a piece of cheesecloth.

2. Mix the vinegar and spice bag in a saucepan, bring to a boil on high heat, remove, and let sit for 25 minutes. Throw away the spice bag.
3. Put the tomatoes, cayenne, and onions in a large saucepan, bring to a boil on high heat, and sit for 20 minutes on reduced heat.
4. Add the infused vinegar, and boil until the vegetables are soft and it begins to thicken. This will take about another 30 minutes.
5. Attach sugar and salt and bring to a boil over medium heat. Reduce the heat, and let it sit for about 45 minutes. Do not puree it.
6. Put the ketchup into the jars, and let the jars sit in a water bath for about 15 minutes.
7. Let cool completely before storing.

Nutrition:

Calories: 314

Protein: 0.9g

Carbs: 81.1g

Fat: 0.2g

Sugar: 77.6g

Chapter 8.   Marmalades

126.   Lemon Honey Marmalade

Preparation time: 10 minutes   **Cooking time:** 40 minutes   **Servings:** 5 pints jar

Ingredients:

- 8 cups lemons, chopped
- 6 oz. liquid pectin
- 1 ½ cups water
- 4 cups sugar
- 2 cups honey

Directions:

1. Add lemons, sugar, water, and honey in a saucepan and bring to boil over medium heat.
2. Reduce heat and simmer for 30 minutes.
3. Add pectin and boil for 5 minutes. Stir constantly.
4. Remove pan from heat. Ladle the marmalade into the jars. Leave ½ inch headspace. Remove air bubbles.
5. Secure jars with lids and process in a boiling water bath for 10 minutes.
6. Remove jars from the water bath and let it cool completely.
7. Check seals of jars. Label and store.

Nutrition:

Calories: 468

Fat: 0.4g

Carbohydrates: 127.5g

Sugar: 116.6g

Protein: 1.7g

Cholesterol: 0mg

127.   Queen Henrietta Maria's 'Marmalade' of Cherries

Preparation time: 25 minutes   **Cooking time:** 40 minutes   **Servings:** 7 pints jar

Ingredients:

- 6 cups cherries (2 lbs.), pitted
- 5½ cups red currants (1 ½ lb.)
- 4 cups raspberries
- Juice of 3 lemons
- 7½ cups granulated sugar

Directions:

1. Clean the jars and lids and keep them warm in a boiling-water canner. In a saucepan, combine the fruit and 1 ¼ Cup water. Bring to a low simmer and boil for 12 minutes, or until the fruit is tender. Cook slowly until the sugar melts, then add the lemon juice.
2. Raise the heat to be high and bring the water to a boil. Skim. Allow cooling for 12 minutes to ensure that the larger pieces of fruit are uniformly distributed.
3. Fill each jar to the top, leaving a 14 in. headspace. At sea level, process the full jars in a boiling-water canner for 10 minutes. Allow cooling before sealing and labeling the jars.

Nutrition:

Carbohydrates: 23g

Fat: 0g

Protein: 0g

Sodium: 2mg

Calories: 88

128.   Carrot Marmalade

Preparation time: 10 minutes   **Cooking time:** 40 minutes   **Servings:** 2 pints jar

Ingredients:

- 2 cups grated carrots
- 2 ½ cups sugar
- 2 cups water
- 1 orange
- 1 lemon

Directions:

1. Shred orange and lemon in a large saucepan.
2. Add remaining ingredients into the saucepan and bring to boil over medium heat.
3. Set heat to low and parboil for 30 minutes or until thickened.
4. Once marmalade is thickened then remove the pan from heat.
5. Ladle the marmalade into the clean and hot jars. Leave ½ inch headspace. Remove air bubbles.
6. Secure jars with lids and process in a boiling water bath for 5 minutes.
7. Remove jars from the water bath and let it cool completely.
8. Check seals of jars. Label and store.

Nutrition:

Calories: 43

Fat: 0g

Carbohydrates: 11.3g

Sugar: 11g

Protein: 0.1g

Cholesterol: 0mg

129.   Strawberry Marmalade

Preparation time: 10 minutes   **Cooking time:** 20 minutes   **Servings:** 4 pints jar

Ingredients:

- 4 cups strawberries, crushed
- 6 cups sugar
- 6 tbsp. pectin
- 1 lemon

Directions:

1. Cut lemon peel and reserved lemon juice and pulp. Add lemon peel in a small pot with water and boil for 5 minutes. Drain lemon peels.
2. Add strawberries, sugar, pectin, lemon peel, lemon juice, and lemon pulp into the large stockpot. Stir well and bring to boil. Stir until sugar is dissolved.
3. Set heat to high and boil for 1 minute. Stir constantly.
4. Remove pot from heat.
5. Ladle the marmalade into the clean and hot jars. Leave ½ inch headspace. Remove air bubbles.
6. Secure jars with lids and process in a boiling water bath for 10 minutes.
7. Remove jars from the water bath and let it cool completely.
8. Check seals of jars. Label and store.

Nutrition:

Calories: 396

Fat: 0.1g

Carbohydrates: 104g

Sugar: 102g

Protein: 0.3g

Cholesterol: 0mg

130.   Strawberry Lemon Marmalade

Preparation time: 5 Minutes   **Cooking time:** 60 Minutes   **Servings:** 4 pints jar

Ingredients:

- 6 cup sugar
- 1 tablespoon lime
- ¼ cup peeled and sliced lemons
- 6 tablespoons classic pectin
- 4 cup crushed strawberries

Directions:

1. Get the canners prepared. Heat jars with simmering water. Don't boil them. Wash the lids with hot soapy water.
2. Mix the lemon peels with water in a pan. Cover the pan. Boil the mixture at medium flame and boil for about 5 minutes until the peel gets softened. Drain the liquid.
3. Now include the lime and strawberries to lemon peel and mix them. Slowly stir the pectin. Heat the mixture at a high flame with occasional stirring.

4. Include sugar and stir until it dissolves. Make the mixture to get boiled for one minute with constant stirring. Remove the flame and skim off the foam if required.
5. Pour the jam into sterilized jars with a spoon. Cover them with lids and seal them.
6. Process all jars in a boiling water canner for about 10 minutes. Remove the jars and let them cool.

Nutrition:

Calories: 149

Carbs: 37.7g

Fat: 0.4g

Protein: 1.3g

131.   Pink Grapefruit Marmalade

Preparation time: 5 Minutes   **Cooking time:** 2 Hours   **Servings:** 3 pints jar

Ingredients:

- 2 grapefruits
- 2½ cups sugar
- 2½ cups brown sugar
- 2 lemons juice

Directions:

1. Place the grapefruit in a pot with enough water so it can float freely.
2. Let them boil for about 2 hours, then let them cool.
3. Slice the grapefruit and mix with the sugars and lemon juice.
4. Put into jars and process for water bath canning for about 10 minutes.
5. Let cool completely before storing.

Nutrition:

Calories: 150

Carbohydrates: 3.3g

Fat: 15.3g

Proteins: 0.5g

132.   Rhubarb Marmalade

Preparation time: 10 minutes   **Cooking time:** 35 minutes   **Servings:** 6 pints jar

Ingredients:

- 6 cups fresh rhubarb, chopped
- 2 medium oranges
- 6 cups sugar

Directions:

1. Grind oranges into the food processor with a peel.
2. Add rhubarb, sugar, and grind oranges into the large saucepan and bring to boil. Reduce heat and simmer for 1 hour.
3. Remove pan from heat. Ladle the marmalade into the jars. Leave ¼ inch headspace.
4. Secure jars with lids and process in a boiling water bath for 10 minutes.
5. Remove jars from the water bath and let it cool completely.
6. Check seals of jars. Label and store.

Nutrition:

Calories: 302

Sugar: 77.7g

Fat: 0.1g

Protein: 0.6g

Carbohydrates: 79.8g

Cholesterol: 0 mg

133.   Peaches and Vanilla Syrup

Preparation time: 15 Minutes   **Cooking time:** 2 Hours   **Servings:** 3 pints jars

Ingredients:

- 5 cups peaches, pureed
- 2 cups sugar
- 2 tablespoons lemon juice
- 2 teaspoons vanilla

Directions:

1. Mix the peach puree with sugar and lemon juice in a medium-sized saucepot and bring to a boil.

2. Let it parboil for 5 minutes, and then add the vanilla.
3. Pour the mixture into jars and seal them.
4. Let your jars sit in a water bath for about 20 minutes before storing.
5. Let cool completely before storing.

Nutrition:

Calories: 37   Carbs: 7.4g

Protein: 1.9g   Fat: 0.8g

134.   Blueberry Marmalade

Preparation time: 10 minutes   **Cooking time:** 45 minutes   **Servings:** 4 pints jar

Ingredients:

- 4 cups blueberries, crushed
- 5 cups sugar
- ⅛ tsp. baking soda
- ¾ cup water

- 1 lemon, peel
- 1 orange, peel
- 6 oz. liquid fruit pectin

Directions:

1. Chop lemon and orange rind and place in pan.
2. Chop lemon and orange pulp and set aside.
3. Add baking soda and ¾ cup water to the pan and bring to boil. Reduce heat and simmer for 10 minutes. Stir frequently.
4. Add lemon and orange pulp, sugar, and blueberries. Return to boil.
5. Set heat to low and parboil for 5 minutes.
6. Set off pan from heat and let it cool for 5-10 minutes.
7. Add pectin and return to boil, stir constantly for 1 minute. Remove from heat.
8. Pour the marmalade into the clean jars. Leave ¼ inch headspace.
9. Seal jars with lids. Set in a water bath canner for 10 minutes.
10. Remove jars from the water bath and let it cool completely.
11. Check seals of jars. Label and store.

Nutrition:

Calories: 352   Sugar: 90g

Fat: 0.2g   Protein: 0.5g

Carbohydrates: 92g   Cholesterol: 0mg

135.   Juicy Mango

Preparation time: 5 minutes   **Cooking time:** 1 hour 10 minutes   **Servings:** 3 pints jar

Ingredients:

- 2 lemons
- 2 mangoes

- 2 cups granulated sugar
- 2 cups water

Directions:

1. Properly wash your mangoes and lemons. Peel and thinly slice them.
2. In a medium pot, place the lemons and water over high heat. Bring the pot to a boil, reduce the heat, and cover it. Let it parboil for 25 minutes while stirring occasionally.
3. Increase the heat to high and mix in the mangoes. Set it back up to a boil while stirring it. Again, you're going to reduce the heat, cover, and let it gently cook for 20 minutes.
4. Stir in the sugar and let it boil for another 15 minutes uncovered. The mixture should have a thick consistency.
5. Pour the mixture into your sterilized jars, close, and tighten properly.

6. Bring your water bath canner to a boil and place the jars inside. Check that everything is correct while it boils again. Place the lid on your canner and begin counting down the 10 minutes processing time.

Nutrition:

Calories: 352

Sugar: 90g

Fat: 0.2g

Protein: 0.5g

Carbohydrates: 92g

---

136.   Strawberry and Blackberry Marmalade

Preparation time: 15 minutes   **Cooking time:** 5 minutes   **Servings:** 3 pints jar

Ingredients:

- 1 lemon
- 1 ¾ cups fresh strawberries, hulled and crushed
- 1 cup fresh blackberries, crushed
- 1 ½ teaspoons freshly squeezed lemon juice
- 3 tablespoons powdered pectin
- 3 ½ cups sugar

Directions:

1. Prepare a hot water bath. Set the jars in it to keep warm. Clean the lids and rings in hot, soapy water, and set aside.
2. Wash the lemon well with warm, soapy water. With a sharp knife, cut away half of the rind from the lemon, removing as much of the pith (white inner membrane) as possible. Slice the rind into thin strips, and then cut the strips into ¼ inch-long pieces.
3. In a small saucepot set over high heat, combine the lemon rind with enough water to cover. Bring to a boil. Strain and reserve the rind.
4. In a medium saucepot set over high heat, combine the strawberries, blackberries, lemon rind, and lemon juice. Slowly stir in the pectin. Set the mixture to a full, rolling boil.
5. Add the sugar. Return the mixture to a full, rolling boiling over high heat. When the jam cannot be stirred down, set a timer for 1 minute and stir constantly. Turn off the heat.
6. With the heat off, stir the marmalade for 1 minute more to ensure even distribution of the rind before filling the jars. Skim off any foam.
7. Ladle the marmalade into the prepared jars, leaving ¼ inch of headspace. Use a nonmetallic utensil to remove any air bubbles. Clean the rims clean and seal with the lids and rings.
8. Bring the jars in a hot water bath for 10 minutes. Set off the heat and let the jars rest in the water bath for 10 minutes.
9. Carefully detach the jars from the hot water canner. Set aside for 12 hours.
10. Check the lids for proper seals. Detach the rings, wipe the jars, name and date them, and transfer to a cupboard or pantry.
11. Refrigerate and use within 3 weeks. Properly secure jars will last in the cupboard for 12 months.

Nutrition:

Calories: 49

Protein: 3.6g

Fat: 0.2g

Sugars: 4.9g

Carbs: 8.7g

---

137.   Grapefruit Marmalade with Vanilla

Preparation time: 25 minutes   **Cooking time:** 60 minutes   **Servings:** 3 pints jar

Ingredients:

- 3 grapefruits
- 3 cups sugar
- 1 whole vanilla bean

Directions:

1. Prepare a hot water bath. Set the jars in it to keep warm. Clean the lids and rings in hot, soapy water, and set aside.

2. Wash the grapefruits well with warm, soapy water. With a sharp knife, remove the grapefruit rind. Stack into piles and slice into strips. Mince the strips.
3. In a small saucepan over medium heat, merge the minced rind with enough water to cover. Bring to a simmer. Cook for 20 minutes, or until tender.
4. While the rind cooks, remove any remaining pith from the grapefruit with your hands or a knife. Working on a bowl to catch the juice, slice along the membranes, removing each grapefruit segment individually. attach the segments to the bowl with the juice. When finished, squeeze the remaining membranes over the bowl to collect any additional juice. Discard the membranes and seeds.
5. Strain the rind, reserving 2 cups of the cooking liquid.
6. In a medium saucepot set over medium-high heat, combine the reserved cooking liquid, sugar, rind, and the grapefruit segments in their juices. Bring to a full, rolling boil. Cook for 35 to 45 minutes until it reaches 220°F (104°C), measured with a candy thermometer.
7. Add the vanilla bean seeds. Turn off the heat. Use the plate test to determine if the marmalade sets. If not, return the pot to the burner and cook in 5-minute increments until it sets to your liking.
8. With the heat off, stir the marmalade for 1 minute to evenly distribute the rind. Skim off any foam.
9. Ladle the marmalade into the prepared jars, leaving ¼ inch of headspace. Use a nonmetallic utensil to remove any air bubbles. Wipe the rims clean and seal using the lids and rings.
10. Set the jars in a hot water bath for 10 minutes. Set off the heat and bring the jars rest in the water bath for 10 minutes.
11. Carefully detach the jars from the hot water canner. Set aside to cool for 12 hours.
12. Check the lids for proper seals. Detach the rings, clean the jars, label and date them, and transfer to a cupboard or pantry.
13. Use within 3 weeks.

Nutrition:

Calories: 149

Carbs: 37.7g

Fat: 0.4g

Protein: 1.3g

138.   Lemon-Rosemary Marmalade

Preparation time: 15 minutes   **Cooking time:** 10 minutes   **Servings:** 6 pints jar

Ingredients:

- 7 medium lemons (about 2 pounds)
- ½ tsp. baking soda, divided
- 7 cups of water
- 4 cups of sugar
- 4 tsp. minced fresh rosemary
- 2 drops yellow food coloring, optional

Directions:

1. Peel lemons into broad strips with a vegetable peeler. Remove the white pit from the peels using a sharp knife. Cut the skins into one quarter of an in. strip
2. Put aside the fruit.
3. In a small bowl, put the lemon strips; add the water and ¼ tsp. baking soda. Bring the water to a boil. - To a boil. Shrink to medium heat. Cook 10 minutes covered; drain. Drain. Remove with baked soda remaining.
4. Cut out the top and bottom of a thin slice of lemons; stand on cutting board lemons straight. Cut the outside membrane of the lemons with a knife. Cut along the membrane of a dish to collect juices every Fruit removal section. To reserve further juice, squeeze the membrane
5. In a Dutch oven, place the piece of the lemon and the saved liquids. Mix in 7 bowls. of water and lemon peel. Bring the water to a boil. Reduce heat; simmer, uncovered, 25 minutes. Add sugar. Bring the water to a boil. - To a boil. Reduce heat; cool, uncovered, stirring periodically 40-50 minutes or until thickened somewhat. Remove from heat; mix rosemary and food coloring if desired.
6. Ladle in 5 heated half pints jar a hot mixture, ¼ in. Clean the rims. Screw on bands until fingertip tight; center lids on jars.

7. Into a canner full of sparkling water, place the jars, making sure they are completely covered. Take a boil and reduce to a frying glass for 10 minutes. Remove and chill the jars. Remove them.

Nutrition:

Carbohydrates: 3g

Fat: 0g

Protein: 0g

Sodium: 182mg

Calories: 14

139. Rhubarb Raisin Marmalade

Preparation time: 25 minutes   **Cooking time:** 10 minutes   **Servings:** 6 pints jar

Ingredients:

- 2 medium oranges
- 1 medium lemon
- 6 cups of sugar
- 6 cups of diced fresh or frozen rhubarb
- 1-½ cups of fresh or frozen strawberries
- Pinch salt
- 1 cup of raisins

Directions:

1. Finely grate the skins of the oranges and lemons; squeeze the juices and set aside. Place the peels, juices, sugar, rhubarb, strawberries, and salt in a Dutch oven and mix well. Cook until sugar is melted, stirring frequently; mix in the raisins. Bring to a full rolling boil, then reduce to a low heat and simmer for 5 minutes, or until the sauce has thickened. Remove the heat from the saucepan and skim out froth that has formed.
2. Ladle heated mixture into hot pints jar with care, allowing a ¼ inch headspace. Air bubbles should be removed, rims should be cleaned, and lids should be adjusted. In a boiling water canner, process for 10 minutes.

Nutrition:

Calories: 314

Protein: 0.9g

Carbs: 81.1g

Fat: 0.2g

Sugar: 77.6g

140. Blueberry Orange Marmalade

Preparation time: 15 minutes   **Cooking time:** 25 minutes   **Servings:** 3 pints jar

Ingredients:

- ½ cup water
- ⅛ teaspoon baking soda
- 1 small orange, peeled and chopped
- 1 small lemon, peeled and chopped
- 2 cups blueberries, crushed
- 2½ cups sugar
- ½ (6-ounce) package liquid fruit pectin

Directions:

1. In a saucepan or cooking pot, merge the water and baking soda.
2. Boil the mixture; cook for about 10 minutes over low heat. Stir continually to prevent scorching.
3. Add the sugar, berries, lemon and orange.
4. Boil the mixture; cook for about 5 minutes over medium-low heat. Stir continually to prevent scorching.
5. Mix in the pectin and simmer for about 1 minutes over medium-low heat until firm and thick. Stir continually to prevent scorching.
6. Spill the hot mixture into pre-sterilized jars directly or with a jar funnel. Keep headspace of ¼ inch from the jar top.
7. To detach tiny air bubbles, insert a nonmetallic spatula and stir the mixture gently.
8. Clean the sealing edges with a damp cloth. Secure the jars with the lids and adjust the bands/rings to seal and prevent any leakage.
9. Set the jars in a hot water bath for 10 minutes.

10. Set the jars in a cool, dry and dark place. Allow them to cool down completely.
11. Store in your refrigerator and use within 10 days.

Nutrition:

Calories: 393

Fat: 0.1g

Carbohydrates: 104.1g

Sugar: 99.8g

Protein: 0.4g

Cholesterol: 0mg

141.   Grapefruit-Lemon Marmalade

Preparation time: 5 Minutes   **Cooking time:** 60 Minutes   **Servings:** 4 pints jar

Ingredients:

- 3 clean grapefruits
- 2 clean medium lemons
- 4 cups water
- 5 cups sugar, granulated

Directions:

1. Cut the grapefruits and lemons into quarters, then slice thinly. Place the fruits and water in a large, heavy-bottomed pot or saucepan. Bring to a boil and cook for about 30 minutes, or until rind is tender.
2. Reduce heat and add the sugar, constantly stirring until the sugar is dissolved completely. Add the ginger and increase heat; cook until it reaches setting point 220 °F.
3. Transfer marmalade to hot sterilized jars, leaving ¼ inch headspace. Cover tightly with lid.
4. Place jars in a hot water bath. Process for 10 minutes. Cool completely at room temperature.
5. Store in a cool, dark place. Keep refrigerated once opened.

Nutrition:

Carbohydrates: 3g

Fat: 0g

Protein: 0g

Sodium: 182mg

Calories: 14

142.   Ginger Flavored Marmalade

Preparation time: 15 Minutes   **Cooking time:** 8 Hours and 35 minutes   **Servings:** 5 half-pints jar

Ingredients:

- 3 ½ cups ginger, fresh and peeled
- 4 cups water, cold
- 5 cups sugar, white
- 1-3 oz. package pectin, liquid variety
- 5 ½ pint canning jars, with lids and jars

Directions:

1. First, place your ginger and water into a large-sized saucepan. Set over medium heat and bring this mixture to a boil.
2. Once your mixture is boiling, reduce the heat to low. Cover and allow to simmer for the next hour and 15 minutes or until your ginger is tender to the touch.
3. Once tender, strain your ginger through a fine-mesh strainer and drain.
4. Place your ginger into a large-sized bowl with your ginger liquid and allow it to cool.
5. Place back into your large-sized saucepan and add in your sugar. Boil for the next minute, making sure you stir constantly.
6. Add in your liquid pectin and reduce the heat to low. Continue to cook for the next 7 minutes and skim off any excess foam formed on the top. Detach from heat and let it cool slightly.
7. Pour the mixture into your canning jars and seal with your lids.
8. Boil the jars in some boiling water for the next 10 minutes. Remove and let it cool slightly before placing it into your fridge. Use whenever you are ready.

Nutrition:

Carbohydrates: 1g

Fat: 0g

Protein: 1g   Calories: 4g
Sodium: 727mg

143.   Apple Marmalade

Preparation time: 15 minutes   **Cooking time:** 30 minutes   **Servings:** 4 pints jar
Ingredients:

- 6 cups apples; peeled, cored, and sliced
- 1 cup water
- 1 tablespoon fresh lemon juice
- 1 (2-ounce) package fruit pectin
- 4 cups white sugar
- 1 lemon, sliced thinly
- 1 teaspoon ground cinnamon

Directions:

1. In a nonreactive saucepan, add chopped apples, water, and lemon juice and bring to a gentle simmer.
2. Cover the saucepan and cook for about 15 minutes, stirring occasionally.
3. Stir in fruit pectin and bring to a full boil, stirring continuously.
4. Add sugar, lemon slices, and cinnamon and again, bring to a full boil, stirring continuously.
5. Boil for about 1 minute, stirring continuously.
6. In 6 (½-pint) hot sterilized jars, divide the marmalade, leaving about ½-inch space from the top.
7. Slide a small knife around the insides of each jar to remove air bubbles.
8. Close each jar with a lid and screw on the ring.
9. Arrange the jars in a boiling water canner and process for about 10 minutes.
10. Remove the jars from water canner and place onto a wood surface several inches apart to cool completely.
11. After cooling with your finger, press the top of each jar's lid to ensure that the seal is tight.
12. The canned marmalade can be stored in the pantry for up to 1 year.

Nutrition:
Calories: 85   Carbs: 22.1g
Fat: 0g   Protein: 0.1g

144.   Strawberry Lemon Marmalade

Preparation time: 15 minutes   **Cooking time:** 20 minutes   **Servings:** 4 pints jar
Ingredients:

- 6 cup sugar
- 1 tbsp. lime
- ¼ cup peeled and sliced lemons
- 6 tbsp. classic pectin
- 4 cup crushed strawberries

Directions:

1. Get the canners prepared. Heat jars with simmering water. Don't boil them. Wash the lids with hot soapy water.
2. Mix the lemon peels with water in a pan. Cover the pan. Boil the mixture at medium flame and let them boil for about 5 minutes, until the peel gets softened. Drain the liquid.
3. Now include the lime and strawberries to lemon peel and mix them. Slowly stir the pectin. Heat the mixture at high flame with occasional stirring.
4. Include sugar and stir until it dissolves. Make the mixture to get boiled for one minute with constant stirring. Remove the flame and skim off the foam if required.
5. Pour the jam into sterilized jars with ladle. Cover them with lids and seal them.
6. Process the jars in boiled water canner for about 10 minutes. Remove the jars and allows them to cool.

Nutrition:
Calories: 40   Protein: 0g
Carbohydrates: 10g   Fats: 0g

145.   Carrot Marmalade

Preparation time: 10 minutes   **Cooking time:** 40 minutes   **Servings:** 3 pints jar

Ingredients:

- 2 cups grated carrots
- 2 ½ cups stevia
- 2 cups water
- 1 orange
- 1 lemon

Directions:

1. Shred orange and lemon in a large saucepan.
2. Add remaining ingredients into the saucepan and bring to boil over medium heat.
3. Set heat to low and parboil for 30 minutes or until thickened.
4. Once marmalade is thickened then remove the pan from heat.
5. Ladle the marmalade into the clean and hot jars. Leave ½-inch headspace. Remove air bubbles.
6. Secure jars with lids and process in a boiling water bath for 5 minutes.
7. Remove jars from the water bath and let it cool completely.
8. Check seals of jars. Label and store.

Nutrition:

Calories: 35

Total Fat: 0g

Carbohydrates: 4g

Proteins: 0g

146.   Carrot, Pineapple, and Orange

Preparation time: 10 minutes   **Cooking time:** 1 hour 20 minutes   **Servings:** 3 pints jar

Ingredients:

- 1 cup shredded carrot
- 2 lemons
- 2 cups chopped orange pulp
- 3 tbsp. pectin
- 1 cup crushed pineapple 8 oz. can crushed and drained
- 2 cups sugar

Directions:

1. Wash your lemons properly to remove any dirt. Peel the rind and cut them into thin strips. Juice your lemons to get approximately ⅓ cup.
2. Place your carrots, lemon peel and juice, orange pulp, pineapple, and sugar in a large pot. Set the heat to medium until the pot boils. Stir and reduce the heat. Simmer for 30 minutes.
3. Mix in the pectin and bring the mixture back to a boil for one minute before removing it from the heat entirely.
4. Place the hot mixture into your sterilized jars, leaving enough room for the headspace. Remove the air bubbles and seal properly.
5. Allow your canner to boil before placing the jars inside. Make sure that they're separated and fully submerged in water. Bring the canner to a boil and close the lids. Start the 10 minutes countdown.
6. When the processing time is finished, take the jars out and set to cool.

Nutrition:

Calories: 40

Carbohydrates: 10g

Protein: 0g

Fats: 0g

147.   Ruby Grapefruit

Preparation time: 20 minutes   **Cooking time:** 35 minutes   **Servings:** 3 pints jar

Ingredients:

- 3 cups of white sugar
- 4 ruby red grapefruits

Directions:

1. Ensure your canning equipment and jars have been sterilized and are ready for the process.
2. Wash and dry your grapefruits properly before using them. Zest 2 of your grapefruits completely and cut the peels of the others into thin strips.
3. Peel the rest of the white parts off the grapefruits and cut them however you desire.
4. In a large pan, place the grapefruit pieces and strips of peel with the sugar. Set the heat to medium-high and continuously stir until it boils.
5. Set the heat to a low setting and mash the fruit pieces to release the juices. Bring the pot to a boil while removing any foam that is produced. Let the mixture cook for 10 minutes, or until it's thick enough to coat the back of a spoon.
6. Stir in the zest pieces and simmer for a further 5 minutes. Set a small amount of the mixture on a plate and freeze it. Check it after 3 minutes and, if it's reached the desired consistency, remove the pot from the heat.
7. Ladle the grapefruit mixture into your jars with a proper headspace. Seal them as directed and get ready to can them.
8. When the water is boiling in your water bath canner, place the jars in and sufficiently surround them with water. Wait for the canner to boil before placing the lid on and starting the 10 minutes processing time.
9. Allow the jars to cool as instructed for canning.

Nutrition:

Calories: 149   Carbs: 37.7g

Fat: 0.4g   Protein: 1.3g

148.   Brilliant Kumquat

Preparation time: 50 minutes   **Cooking time:** 10 minutes   **Servings:** 4 pints jar

Ingredients:

- 1 ¾ lbs. kumquats
- 1 ¾ oz. powdered fruit pectin
- 6 ½ cups sugar
- 1 cup water

Directions:

1. Wash and rinse your kumquats thoroughly. Cut them in half to remove their seeds and then chop the kumquats into fine pieces. A food processor works great. You're looking for a coarse texture.
2. Place a large pot on high heat. Add in the kumquats, water, and pectin. Set the pot to a boil while stirring frequently.
3. Next, mix in the sugar and allow it to boil for another 1 minute. Remove any foam residue from the mixture.
4. Divide the kumquat mixture into your jars evenly while keeping in mind the headspace needed. Remove any air bubbles, seal, and tighten correctly.
5. Bring your water bath canner to a gentle boil. Place the jars inside and check the water levels. Allow the canner to boil and place the cover on top. The processing time from this point is 10 minutes.
6. Take the jars out of your canner and put aside to cool for the suggested time.

Nutrition:

Carbohydrates: 23g   Sodium: 2mg

Fat: 0g   Calories: 88

Protein: 0g

149.   Lavender and Lemon

Preparation time: 50 minutes   **Cooking time:** 10 minutes   **Servings:** 8 half-pints jar

Ingredients:

- 2 tsp. dried culinary lavender
- 2 lbs. lemons

- 8 cups granulated sugar

Directions:

1. Prepare your lemons by washing and peeling them. Set aside the actual lemon fruit and cut the lemon peel into thin strips.
2. Juice your lemons and remove any seeds that might have fallen into the juice. Wrap the seeds and leftover lemon membrane in a cheesecloth to infuse into the mixture.
3. Place the peel strips, juice, and cheesecloth bag into a large pot. Pour in the water, stir, and bring to a boil. Once it's softly boiling, turn down the heat and simmer the lemon mixture for 1 ½ - 2 hours.
4. Take the cheesecloth bag out and let the liquid cool for 5 minutes. While it's cooling, you can prepare your jars and equipment.
5. When you can safely handle the cheesecloth, squeeze as much as you can out of it and into the lemon mixture. This step adds more pectin into the marmalade, which it needs.
6. Lastly, stir in the lavender and sugar until it's fully dissolved. Place the pot back onto medium-high heat to boil for 15 minutes. Continue cooking it until the mixture reaches the desired consistency. Remove the foam that forms on the top and set aside to cool for another 15 minutes.
7. Separate the mixture into your jars and create a good headspace. Seal and tighten as stated.
8. As your water bath canner boils, lower the jars into it carefully and make sure that they're separated enough. Check that the water fully covers them as it boils again. Cover and start the processing time of 10 minutes.
9. When it's finished, set the jars aside to cool completely.

Nutrition:

Carbohydrates: 3g   Sodium: 182mg

Fat: 0g   Calories: 14

Protein: 0g

150.   Lemon and Ginger

Preparation time: 50 minutes   **Cooking time:** 10 minutes   **Servings:** 7 half-pints jar

Ingredients:

- ½ tsp. baking soda
- 1 cup grated fresh ginger
- 6 small lemons
- 1 ¾ oz. powdered fruit pectin
- 6 ½ cups sugar
- 2 ½ cups water

Directions:

1. Prepare your lemons by washing them properly and peel them. Slice the peels into thin strips.
2. Remove the rest of the white pith from the lemons. Working over a bowl, segment the lemons and make sure you save most of the juice. Squeeze the segments into the bowl to release as much juice as possible from them. Remove the seeds and the membrane from the juice.
3. Set a pot over medium heat with the water, baking soda, and lemon peels in it. Set it to a boil and then reduce the heat to simmer for 5 minutes until the peel is tender, then remove the pot from the heat.
4. Add in 1 cup of the juice with the ginger and stir. Next, briskly whisk in the pectin to make sure it dissolves properly.
5. Set the pot back onto high heat and bring it to a boil. Stir consistently and add the sugar while it continues to boil.
6. Once the sugar has processed, allow it to boil for another minute before taking it off the heat and removing any residual foam.
7. Equally divide the mixture into your sterilized jars with some headspace. Properly close them as stated in the process directions.
8. Process the jars into the boiling water of your water bath canner. Ensure there is enough space and water. Set the water to a boil again and close the lid. Start counting down the processing time of 10 minutes.

9. Once done, remove the jars and allow them to cool for the appropriate time frame.

Nutrition:

Carbohydrates: 23g

Fat: 0g

Protein: 0g

Sodium: 2mg

Calories: 88

Chapter 9.   Relish and Salads

151.   Jalapeno Pineapple Relish

Preparation time: 10 minutes   **Cooking time:** 40 minutes   **Servings:** 5 pints jar

Ingredients:

- 8 cups pineapple, diced
- 4 jalapeno peppers, seeded and diced
- 1 cup vinegar
- 1 onion, diced
- 1 ½ tsp. ground coriander
- ½ cup sugar
- ½ cup water
- Salt

Directions:

1. Add jalapeno, pineapple, and onion into the food processor and process for 2-3 times to finely chop.
2. Add pineapple mixture into the large pot.
3. Add remaining ingredients and stir well and cook over medium heat. Bring to boil.
4. Reduce heat, and simmer for 25 minutes.
5. Ladle relish into the jars. Leave ½ inch headspace.
6. Seal jar with lids. Set in a water bath canner for 15 minutes.
7. Remove jars from the water bath and let it cool completely.
8. Check seals of jars. Label and store.

Nutrition:

Calories: 144   Sugar: 30g

Fat: 0.4g   Protein: 1g

Carbohydrates: 35g   Cholesterol: 0 mg

152.   Onion Relish

Preparation time: 10 minutes   **Cooking time:** 35 minutes   **Servings:** 6 pints jar

Ingredients:

- 8 cups onion, sliced
- 1 cup vinegar
- ¼ tsp. mustard seeds
- 1 ½ cups sugar
- 1 tsp. salt

Directions:

1. Add sliced onion to the boiling water and cook for 5 minutes. Drain well and set aside.
2. Attach remaining ingredients to the saucepan and bring to boil.
3. Add onion to the saucepan and simmer for 5 minutes.
4. Pack onion to the clean jars. Leave ½ inch headspace.
5. Seal jar with lids. Set in a water bath canner for 10 minutes.
6. Remove jars from the water bath and let it cool completely.
7. Check seals of jars. Label and store.

Nutrition:

Calories: 255   Sugar: 55g

Fat: 0.3g   Protein: 1.7g

Carbohydrates: 65g   Cholesterol: 0 mg

153.   Sandwich Relish

Preparation time: 10 minutes   **Cooking time:** 35 minutes   **Servings:** 4 pints jar

Ingredients:

- 20 red chilies, stemmed, halved, seeded, and coarsely chopped
- 10 green chilies, stemmed, halved, seeded, and coarsely chopped
- 1 tablespoon canning salt
- 2 pounds onions, peeled and chopped
- 1 ½ cups apple cider vinegar
- 1 ½ cups sugar

Directions:

1. Set a hot water bath. Bring the jars in it to keep warm. Clean the rings and lids in hot, soapy water, and set aside.
2. In a food processor, process the chilies into a coarse paste. Transfer to a bowl. Add the canning salt and enough boiling water to cover. Let stand for 10 minutes. Drain.
3. In a preserving pot or saucepot set over medium heat, mix the ground chilis and onions. Add the vinegar and sugar. Allow to come to a boil. Boil for 20 minutes.
4. Spoon the relish into your jars, leaving ½ inch of headspace.
5. Place jars in your hot water bath and process for 15 minutes. Turn the heat off and allow the jars to rest in the water bath for 10 minutes.
6. Carefully detach the jars from the hot water canner. Set aside to cool for 12 hours.
7. Check the lids for proper seals. Detach the rings, wipe the jars, label and date them, and transfer to a cupboard or pantry.
8. Properly secure jars will last in the cupboard for 12 months. Once opened, refrigerate and consume within 1 month.

Nutrition:

Calories: 49

Fat: 0.2g

Carbs: 8.7g

Protein: 3.6g

Sugars: 4.9g

154.   Dill Pickle Relish

Preparation time: 2 hours 15 minutes

Cooking time: 25 minutes

Servings: 7 pints jar

Ingredients:

- ¼ cup red bell pepper
- 9 lbs. pickling cucumbers
- 2 tbsp. dill seed
- 1 ½ cups diced white onion
- ½ cup pickling salt
- 1 tbsp. sugar
- 2 tsp. turmeric
- 4 cups water
- 1 cup apple cider vinegar
- 3 cups white vinegar

Directions:

1. Wash your cucumber and cut the ends off. Slice the cucumbers into 8 parts and remove the seeds from them, then cut the slices into 1-2-inch pieces.
2. Using a food processor or blender of your choice, roughly pulse the cucumbers in separate batches. Set them in a bowl with the salt and turmeric and mix. Pour water over the mixture, cover, and set it aside to brine for 2 hours.
3. Set the cucumber in a colander to drain and squeeze them to release any leftover liquid.
4. Wash the onion and pepper before dicing and add them to a large pot.
5. Place the pot on medium heat. Attach in the rest of the ingredients, including the cucumbers, and bring the pot to a boil.
6. Set the heat and let the mixture cook for 10 minutes.
7. Pour your relish into your prepared and sterilized jars, ensuring there's enough headspace. Close and tighten the jars correctly.
8. Set the jars in the boiling water of your canner. Make sure they're adequately spaced apart, and that there's enough water to cover them. Wait for the canner to boil again before closing it and starting the 15 minutes processing time.

9. When it's finished, remove the jars and store them for cooling.

Nutrition:

Calories: 37

Carbs: 7.4g

Protein: 1.9g

Fat: 0.8g

155. Chile Relish with Onion

Preparation time: 20 minutes **Cooking time:** 20 minutes **Servings:** 6 pints jar

Ingredients:

- 20 red chilies, stemmed, halved, seeded, and coarsely chopped
- 10 green chilies, stemmed, halved, seeded, and coarsely chopped
- 1 tablespoon canning salt
- 2 pounds (907 g) onions, peeled and chopped
- 1 ½ cups apple cider vinegar
- 1 ½ cups sugar

Directions:

1. Set a hot water bath. Bring the jars in it to keep warm. Clean the lids and rings in hot, soapy water, and set aside.
2. In a food processor, process the chilies into a coarse paste. Transfer to a bowl. Add the canning salt and enough boiling water to cover. Let stand for 10 minutes. Drain.
3. In a preserving pot or saucepot set over medium-high heat, mix the ground chiles and onions. Add the vinegar and sugar. Bring to a boil. Boil for 20 minutes.
4. Ladle the relish into the prepared jars, leaving ½ inch of headspace.
5. Set the jars in a hot water bath for 15 minutes. Set off the heat and let the jars rest in the water bath for 10 minutes.
6. Carefully detach the jars from the hot water canner. Set aside to cool for 12 hours.
7. Check the lids for proper seals. Detach the rings, wipe the jars, label and date them, and transfer to a cupboard or pantry, use within 1 month.

Nutrition:

Carbohydrates: 1g

Fat: 0g

Protein: 1g

Sodium: 727mg

Calories: 4

156. Cucumber and Bell Pepper Relish

Preparation time: 15 minutes **Cooking time:** 10 minutes **Servings:** 4 half pints jar

Ingredients:

- 3 cups diced pickling cucumbers
- ¾ cup finely sliced red bell pepper
- ¾ cup finely chopped green bell pepper
- 1 celery stalk, finely chopped
- 1 jalapeño pepper, finely chopped
- 3 tablespoons pickling salt
- 1 ½ cups white vinegar
- ⅓ cup sugar
- 1 tablespoon chopped garlic
- ¾ teaspoon dried thyme

Directions:

1. In a large bowl, merge the cucumbers, red bell pepper, green bell pepper, celery, jalapeño, and pickling salt. Cover with a clean kitchen towel. Let stand at room. Drain in a colander and rinse thoroughly.
2. Set a hot water bath. Bring the jars in it to keep warm. Clean the lids and rings in hot, soapy water, and set aside.
3. In a saucepot set over medium-high heat, merge the white vinegar and sugar. Bring to a boil, swirling until the sugar dissolves.
4. Add the drained vegetables, garlic, and thyme. Return the mixture to a boil.
5. Ladle the relish into the prepared jars, leaving ½ inch of headspace.

6. Set the jars in a hot water bath for 10 minutes. Set off the heat and set the jars rest in the water bath.
7. Carefully detach the jars from the hot water canner. Set aside for 12 hours.
8. Check the lids for proper seals. Remove the rings, clean the jars, label and date them, and transfer to a cupboard or pantry.
9. Refrigerate any jars that don't seal properly and use within 2 months. Properly secure jars will last in the cupboard for 12 months.

Nutrition:

Calories: 43

Fat: 0g

Carbohydrates: 11.3g

Sugar: 11g

Protein: 0.1g

Cholesterol: 0mg

157.   Zucchini Relish with Bell Pepper

Preparation time: 15 minutes   **Cooking time:** 15 minutes   **Servings:** 4 pints jar

Ingredients:

- 4 cups finely diced zucchini
- 2 cups finely chopped red and/or green bell peppers
- 1 cup finely chopped onion
- 2 tablespoons pickling salt
- 2 cups white vinegar
- 1 cup sugar
- 2 tablespoons prepared horseradish
- 1 teaspoon mustard seed

Directions:

Day 1

1. In a large bowl, merge the zucchini, bell peppers, onion, and pickling salt.
2. Cover with a clean kitchen towel. Let stand at room for 12 hours, or overnight.

Day 2

3. Drain the vegetables in a colander and rinse thoroughly. With clean hands, press out any excess water.
4. Prepare a hot water bath. Set the jars in it to keep warm. Clean the lids and rings in hot, soapy water, and set aside.
5. In a medium saucepot set over medium-high heat, combine the white vinegar, sugar, horseradish, and mustard seed. Bring to a boil, swirling until the sugar dissolves.
6. Add the drained vegetables. Return the mixture to a boil. Reduce the heat to low. Simmer for 10 minutes.
7. Ladle the relish into the prepared jars, leaving ¼ inch of headspace. Use a nonmetallic utensil to free any air bubbles. Clean the rims clean and seal with the lids and rings.
8. Set the jars in a hot water bath for 10 minutes. Set off the heat and let the jars rest in the water bath.
9. Carefully detach the jars from the hot water canner. Set to cool for 12 hours.
10. Check the lids for proper seals. Remove the rings, wipe the jars, name and date them, and bring to a cupboard or pantry.
11. Refrigerate any jars that don't secure properly and use within 2 months. Properly secure the jars will last in the cupboard for 12 months.

Nutrition:

Calories: 36.4

Total fat: 0.13g

Carbs: 8.36g

Protein: 1.17g

Sugars: 1g

158.   Sweet Onion Relish

Preparation time: 45 minutes   **Cooking time:** 35 minutes   **Servings:** 4 pints jar

Ingredients:

- 1 tbsp. red chili flakes
- 1 tbsp. mustard seeds

- 5 lbs. sweet onions
- 2 tbsp. salt
- 1 cup granulated sugar
- ½ tsp. turmeric
- 2 cups apple cider vinegar

Directions:
1. Place your onions in a food processor or blender and process them. Mix the onions and salt in a large bowl, massage them, and let it sit for 30 minutes.
2. After 30 minutes, drain the onions and squeeze them to remove any excess liquid.
3. Place all your ingredients in a large pot over medium heat. Set it to come to a boil for 15-20 minutes. The mixture should become soft and thick.
4. Ladle the mixture into your prepared jars. Make sure there's enough headspace before sealing as instructed.
5. Set the jars in the boiling water of your canner. They should be completely covered by the water, and let it come back to a boil. Seal the cover and start the processing time of 15 minutes.
6. Remove, cool, and store properly.

Nutrition:

Carbohydrates: 23g

Fat: 0g

Protein: 0g

Sodium: 2mg

Calories: 88

---

159.   Beet Relish

Preparation time: 15 minutes   **Cooking time:** 20 minutes   **Servings:** 4 pints jar

Ingredients:
- 1 quart chopped, cooked beets
- 2 quart chopped cabbage
- 1 cup chopped onion
- 1 cup chopped sweet red pepper
- 1½ cups sugar
- 1 tbsp. prepared horseradish
- 1 tbsp. pickling salt
- 3 cups white vinegar

Directions:
1. Combine all the fixings in a large pot. Slowly simmer within 10 minutes. Boil, then quickly pack hot into hot jars, leaving ¼ inch of headspace.
2. Place in a bath canner and process for 15 minutes.

Nutrition:

Calories: 34

Fat: 0g

Carbs: 8g

Protein: 0g

---

160.   Chow-Chow Relish

Preparation time: 15 minutes   **Cooking time:** 40 minutes   **Servings:** 4 pints jar

Ingredients:
- 1 medium head cabbage, chopped
- 6 medium onions
- 6 sweet green peppers, remove seeds and ribs
- 6 sweet red peppers, remove seeds and ribs
- 2 quarts hard green tomatoes
- ¼ cup pickling salt
- 2 tbsp. prepared mustard
- 1½ quarts white vinegar
- 2½ cups sugar
- 1½ tsp. ground ginger
- 2 tbsp. mustard seed
- 1 tbsp. celery seed
- 1 tbsp. mixed whole pickling spice

Directions:
1. Chop all vegetables in your meat grinder using a coarse blade. Put with salt, then cover. Let it stand in cool place overnight. Drain.

2. In large pot, mix mustard with small amount of vinegar; add remaining vinegar, sugar, and spices. Let it boil, then simmer within 30 minutes. Add vegetables. Simmer for about 10 minutes.
3. Package the hot relish into sterilized, hot jars, allowing ¼ inch of headspace. Be sure liquid covers vegetables.
4. Place in a bath canner and process for 10 minutes.

Nutrition:

Calories: 15   Carbs: 0g

Fat: 0g   Protein: 0g

161.   Corn Relish

Preparation time: 15 minutes   **Cooking time:** 30 minutes   **Servings:** 6 pints jar

Ingredients:

- 9 cups fresh sweet corn, cut from ears
- 2 cups chopped onions
- 1 cup chopped green peppers, remove stems, seeds, and ribs
- ½ cup chopped red peppers, remove stems, seeds, and ribs
- 1 cup sugar
- 2 tbsp. salt
- 1½ tbsps. celery seed
- 1½ tbsps. mustard seed
- 1 tbsp. turmeric
- 3 cups cider vinegar

Directions:

1. Combine chopped vegetables, sugar, salt, spices, plus vinegar and let it boil.
2. Simmer within 15 minutes, covered, stirring occasionally to prevent scorching. Set hot relish into hot, sterilized jars, leaving ¼ inch of headspace.
3. Place in a bath canner and process for 15 minutes.

Nutrition:

Calories: 40   Protein: 0g

Carbohydrates: 10g   Fats: 0g

162.   Apple Relish

Preparation time: 15 minutes   **Cooking time:** 20 minutes   **Servings:** 4 pints jar

Ingredients:

- 4 lbs. apples, cut into eighths
- 3 quarts water
- 1¼ cups white vinegar, divided
- 1 cup sugar
- ½ cup light corn syrup
- ⅔ cup water
- 2 tsp. whole cloves
- 1½ sticks cinnamon

Directions:

1. Put your apple slices in a bowl with 3 quarts water plus 4 tablespoons of vinegar to prevent darkening.
2. Mix the sugar, corn syrup, rest of vinegar, ⅔ cup water, cloves, plus cinnamon, broken into pieces in your pot. Heat-up to boiling. Drain apples and add to pot.
3. Cover and boil 3 minutes, stirring occasionally. Set hot relish into hot, sterilized jars, leaving ¼ inch of headspace, filling with syrup, leaving ¼ inch of headspace.
4. Set in a water bath canner and process for 10 minutes.

Nutrition:

Calories: 53.1   Carbs: 15.8g

Fat: 0.2g   Protein: 0.3g

163.   Elderberry Relish

Preparation time: 15 minutes   **Cooking time:** 20 minutes   **Servings:** 4 pints jar

Ingredients:

- 3 pints ripe elderberries, stemmed
- 1½ pints white vinegar
- 1½ cups sugar
- 1 tbsp. cinnamon
- 1 tbsp. allspice
- 1 tbsp. cloves
- ¼ tsp. cayenne pepper

Directions:

1. Mix the elderberries to vinegar then simmer to soften. Press your berries through sieve then return to vinegar. Add sugar plus spices and simmer until it begins to thicken.
2. Stir frequently to prevent scorching. Set hot relish into hot, sterilized jars, leaving ¼ inch of headspace. Process within 10 minutes in a water bath canner.

Nutrition:

Calories: 50

Fat: 0g

Carbs: 0g

Protein: 0g

164. Tasty Onion and Pepper Relish

Preparation time: 15 Minutes

Cooking time: 5 Hours and 10 Minutes

Servings: 74 pints jar

Ingredients:

- 3 onions, large and sliced thinly
- 8 green bell peppers, sliced into thin strips
- 3 Jalapeño Peppers, seeded and minced
- 6 tablespoons spices, pickled variety
- 2 cups sugar, white
- 1 teaspoon salt, for taste
- 2 cups vinegar, apple cider variety

Directions:

1. Place all your ingredients into a large-sized saucepan.
2. Bring this mixture to a boil over high heat.
3. Detach from heat and let it cool completely.
4. Pour the mixture into your canning jars and seal with your lids.
5. Boil the jars in some boiling water for the next 10 minutes. Remove and let it cool slightly before placing it into your fridge. Use whenever you are ready.

Nutrition:

Calories: 85

Fat: 0g

Carbs: 22.1g

Protein: 0.1g

165. Rummage Style Relish

Preparation time: 5 Minutes

Cooking time: 13 Hours and 25 minutes

Servings: 25 half pints

Ingredients:

- 8 cups green tomatoes, cored and finely chopped
- 4 cups red tomatoes, peeled, cored, and finely chopped
- 4 cups cabbage, roughly chopped
- 3 cups onion, finely sliced
- 2 cups cucumber, fresh and finely chopped
- 1 cup bell pepper, green in color, and finely chopped
- 1 cup bell pepper, red and finely chopped
- ½ cups salt, to taste
- 4 cups brown sugar, light and packed
- 1 tablespoon celery seed
- 1 tablespoon cinnamon, ground variety
- 1 tablespoon mustard seed
- 1 teaspoon ginger, ground variety
- 2 garlic cloves, minced
- ½ teaspoons cloves, ground variety
- 2 quarts vinegar

Directions:

1. First, use a large-sized bowl and mix your first 7 ingredients until thoroughly combined. Season with your salt and allow to sit for the next 12 to 14 hours. After this time, drain and rinse under some running water.
2. Then use a large-sized pot and mix your remaining ingredients until thoroughly combined.
3. Set over medium heat and set your mixture to a boil, stirring thoroughly to dissolve your sugar.
4. Allow simmering for the next 10 minutes before adding in your vegetable.
5. Continue to simmer for the next 30 minutes. Detach from heat and let it cool slightly.
6. Pour the mixture into your canning jars and seal with your lids.
7. Boil the jars in some boiling water for the next 10 minutes. Remove and let it cool slightly before placing it into your fridge. Use whenever you are ready.

Nutrition:

Calories: 352

Fat: 0.2g

Carbohydrates: 92g

Sugar: 90g

Protein: 0.5g

---

166.   Jalapeno Pepper Relish

Preparation time: 14 minutes   **Cooking time:** 5 minutes   **Servings:** 8 pints jar

Ingredients:

- 5 pounds of finely chopped jalapeño peppers
- 2 cups of sugar
- 4 cups of white vinegar
- ½ cup of cilantro leaves (optional)

Directions:

1. In a food processor, finely slice the peppers. Don't turn them into pureed mush; make them the consistency of a relish.
2. In a large pot, stir the sugar into the vinegar and bring it to a boil. Immediately turn off the heat once the boil is achieved.
3. Use your food processor to slice the cilantro leaves; if you are using them, stir them into your chopped peppers.
4. Ladle the uncooked peppers and cilantro into your canning jars, then spoon the liquid over the mixture, allowing ½ inch of headspace.
5. Bring the jars in a water bath canner for 10 minutes, adjusting for altitude.

Nutrition:

Calories: 36.1

Fat: 0g

Carbohydrates: 10g

Proteins: 0g

---

167.   Spicy Beet Relish

Preparation time: 1 hour   **Cooking time:** 15 minutes   **Servings:** 3 pints jar

Ingredients:

- 4 lbs. fresh beets
- 1 cup sugar
- 1 cup cider vinegar
- 2 tbsp. horseradish, grated and peeled
- 2 tsp. canning salt
- ¼ tsp. pepper
- ½ tsp. cayenne pepper

Directions:

1. Firstly, scrub beets and trim the tops of the beets. Place it into the Dutch oven and cover with water. Bring to a boil, about 45-60 minutes. Remove from water. Let cool it. Peel and shred beets.
2. Mix the vinegar and sugar into the Dutch oven and cook until sugar is dissolved. Add cayenne pepper, salt, horseradish, and shredded beets and bring to a boil.
3. Place hot mixture into the jars. Remove any air bubbles. Wipe rims.

4. Place lids on the jars. Add water into the water bath canner and bring to a boil. Place jars into the water bath canner and bring to a boil. Add more boiled water if required.
5. Cover the water bath canner and process for 15 minutes. Remove the jars from the water bath canner. Let cool it. Make sure that the seal is tight.

Nutrition:

Calories: 170

Fat: 3g

Carbs: 23g

Protein: 14g

168.   Sweet Relish

Preparation time: 35 minutes   **Cooking time:** 35 minutes   **Servings:** 3 pints jar

Ingredients:

- Finely chopped cucumber, 4 cups
- Sweet peppers, diced finely, 2 cups (red or yellow peppers can be used)
- Sea salt, ¼ cup
- Chopped onion, about 2 cups
- Sugar, granulated, 3 ½ cups
- Cider vinegar, 2 cups
- Mustard seed, one tablespoon
- Celery seeds, one tablespoon

Directions:

1. Place the chopped cucumbers into a food processor or blender and pulse them until they are fine and evenly chopped. Measure at least four cups and add them to a bowl. Add the chopped sweet peppers into the blender, ensuring the seeds are removed, then pulse in the same way as the cucumber pieces, and add them to the cucumbers in the large bowl. Repeat the same process with the onions until they are finely chopped.
2. Combine all the ingredients and mix well. Remove two cups of the blend and add salt to the vegetables and continue stirring.
3. Cover the mixture with ice water and place the bowl aside for two hours, then drain in a sieve or colander and wash well. Press to remove any excess liquid. Pour the sugar, celery seed, vinegar, and mustard seed in a large pot and cook until it boils on medium-high heat. Transfer the drained vegetables into the pot and simmer on low for about ten minutes.
4. Scoop the hot relish into the jars, allowing for a space of ½ inch at the top. Attach the lids and rings to each jar and tighten. Set the jars in a water bath canner and cover one inch of water over all of them, then process for 15 minutes. When this process is done, remove and cool before storing it in the pantry.

Nutrition:

Carbohydrates: 3g

Sodium: 182mg

Fat: 0g

Calories: 14

Protein: 0g

169.   Zucchini Relish

Preparation time: 45 minutes   **Cooking time:** 35 minutes   **Servings:** 3 pints jar

Ingredients:

- Zucchini, chopped finely, 4 cups
- Bell peppers, diced, 2 cups
- Onions finely chopped, 2 cups
- Pickling salt, ¼ cup
- Apple cider vinegar, 2 cups
- Cane or raw sugar, 3 ½ cups (you may use less sugar if desired)
- Celery seeds, one tablespoon
- Yellow mustard, two teaspoons

Directions:

1. To prepare the vegetables, finely dice the peppers, zucchini, and onions and place in a large bowl.
2. Attach a light sprinkling of salt over the vegetables and mix to blend. Cover the top with crushed ice cubes and water and set aside the blend for about two hours. Prepare the jars by sterilizing them:

clean thoroughly with soap and water, then rinse well. Bring them in a water bath canner and add water to cover the jars, boiling them for 10 minutes to remove any bacteria, then remove with a lifter and keep them warm on the stovetop until they are ready to use.

3. To cook the relish, drain the iced vegetables after two hours and rinse to remove excess salt. Add in the sugar, mustard seed, celery seed, and vinegar into the large cooking pot. Set the mixture to a boil on medium-high heat and add in the vegetables. Once the boiling point is reached, continue to cook for 10 minutes, then remove the warm jars and scoop the mixture into them, allowing for ½ inch at the top. Use a funnel to ensure none of the relish spills and wipe the rim and outside of the jars before securing the lids on top.

4. Set the jars in a water bath canner and boil to process for about 10 minutes, leaving a space of two inches between them. The water inside the canner should cover at least one inch over all the jars. After the processing is done, shut off the heat and let the canner sit to cool for about 5-7 minutes. Prepare a kitchen towel over the counter and use a jar lifter to remove each jar from the canner. Allow the jars to cool.

5. At some point during the process, you'll hear a popping sound, which means the lids have sealed. This can also be checked by pushing the center of the top gently. If it flexes or moves up and down, this means the seal didn't work, and it should be refrigerated for use within a few days. If the jars seal successfully, store up to one year in a dark, cool place.

Nutrition:

Calories: 82

Protein: 0 g

Fiber: 0 g

Fat: 0 g

Carbs: 82g

170. Spicy Corn Relish

Preparation time: 15 minutes   **Cooking time:** 35 minutes   **Servings:** 4 pints jar

Ingredients:

- Fresh corn on the cob (about 18)
- Red bell peppers, sliced, 2 cups
- 1½ cups of diced green peppers
- Jalapeno, ½ cup chopped finely (optional)
- Crushed garlic, about 2-3 cloves

- Sea salt, two tablespoons
- Dried mustard powder, four teaspoons
- Brown sugar, ⅔ cups
- Cider vinegar, 4 cups
- 1 cup of water

Directions:

1. To prepare the jars, sterilize a minimum of 10-pints jar (or as many as you can). Shuck the corn and remove the silks from the kernels.

2. This is best to perform against a cutting board, carefully, with a sharp knife. Transfer the kernels into a large cooking pot, preferably stainless steel. Add all the other ingredients into the pot and stir well, then bring the contents to a boil.

3. Continue to mix on occasion until the mixture reaches the boiling point, then reduce to medium-low and simmer for about 18-20 minutes.

4. Set the sterilized jars near the stove and gently scoop the corn relish, while it's hot, with a ladle or large spoon into each jar. Allow for ½ inch at the top of each jar and remove any air bubbles inside.

5. Adjust the level of the relish in each jar and ensure that there is no excess liquid on the rim or edges of the jars. Clean this area thoroughly with a paper towel lightly dampened with vinegar. Affix the lids and close them tightly.

6. Place then in the water bath canner and cover them completely, with at least one inch of water over the jars. Bring the canner to a boil, cover, and then process for 15-16 minutes.

7. Remove from the heat and remove the lid to the canner and allow the jars of relish to settle for about 5-7 minutes before transferring them onto a clean cloth or wire rack.

8. All the jars to cool this way, at room temperature, for up to twenty-four hours. After they have cooled, remove the rings from the lids and wipe the jars well. Place them in a cellar or pantry (away from natural light) for up to one year.

Nutrition:

Calories: 255

Fat: 0.3g

Carbohydrates: 65g

Sugar: 55g

Protein: 1.7g

Cholesterol: 0 mg

171.   Zesty Pickled Jalapeno Relish Recipe

Preparation time: 15 minutes   **Cooking time:** 30 minutes   **Servings:** 4 pints jar

Ingredients:

- Jalapeno peppers, about three pounds in total
- Bell peppers, one pound
- Garlic, six cloves
- Onion, 2-3 medium
- Vinegar, 2 cups
- 1 cup of water
- Sea salt, two tablespoons

- Yellow mustard, one teaspoon (or spicy mustard)
- Celery seed, ½ teaspoon
- Cumin (crushed or powder), two teaspoons
- Apple cider vinegar, one cup
- 2 cups of regular vinegar

Directions:

1. When preparing this recipe, it is recommended to wear gloves to protect your skin from the heat of jalapeno peppers, especially when removing seeds and chopping them. Divide the peppers in half and detach the seeds, then continues to dice the jalapeno peppers into fine pieces.
2. Chop and dice both the onion and the garlic and combine with the jalapeno peppers. Transfer all the ingredients into a large stockpot and add in the apple cider vinegar, regular vinegar, salt, cumin, mustard, celery seed, and water.
3. Warmth on the stovetop and bring to a boil on high medium-high heat, then cook for a couple of minutes before reducing to low and cover to cook for another 18-20 minutes.
4. Using a large spoon or ladle, set the prepared relish into sterilized jars and allow for a space of ½ at the top, then remove the air and tighten with the lid and ring. Process in a water bath canner for about 10-12 minutes, then allow the jars to cool and store in a pantry or cold, dark place.

Nutrition:

Calories: 82

Protein: 0g

Fiber: 0g

Fat: 0g

Carbs: 8

172.   Sweet Corn Relish

Preparation time: 15 minutes   **Cooking time:** 40 minutes   **Servings:** 6 pints jar

Ingredients:

- 24 ears corn, husks removed
- 4 celery ribs, chopped
- 2 onions, chopped
- 2-3 tomatoes, chopped
- 4 green bell peppers, chopped
- 2 jalapenos chopped, ribs and seeds removed

- 1 ½ cups granulated sugar
- ¼ cup salt
- 2 tsp. turmeric
- 1 tbsp. celery seed
- 2 tsp. dry mustard
- 5 cups vinegar

Directions:

1. Detach kernels from the cob and place them into the pot. Then, add jalapenos, celery, tomatoes, onions, and peppers.
2. Combine dry mustard, celery seed, turmeric, salt, and sugar into the bowl. Then, add the mixture to the pot and stir well.
3. Reduce the flame and simmer for 40 minutes.
4. Place mixture into the hot and sterilized jars.
5. Remove any air bubbles. Wipe rims.
6. Place lids on the jars. Add water into the water bath canner and bring to a boil. Place jars into the water bath canner and bring to a boil. Add more boiled water if required.
7. Cover the water bath canner and process for 15 minutes. Remove the jars from the water bath canner. Let cool it. Make sure that the seal is tight.

Nutrition:

Calories: 149

Fat: 0.4g

Carbs: 37.7g

Protein: 1.3g

173. Zucchini Squash Relish

Preparation time: 40 minutes   **Cooking time:** 15 minutes   **Servings:** 7 pints jar

Ingredients:

- 2 ½ lbs. zucchini, chopped
- 1 lb. red bell pepper, chopped
- 2 ½ lbs. yellow squash, chopped
- ½ cup sweet onion, diced
- 2 ½ cups granulated sugar
- 1 ½ cups cider vinegar
- ½ cup rice vinegar
- 4 tsp. mustard seeds
- 2 tsp. celery seeds
- 2 tsp. kosher salt

Directions:

1. Add onion, bell pepper, yellow squash, and zucchini into the blender and blend until chopped.
2. Add salt, celery seeds, mustard seeds, rice vinegar, cider vinegar, and sugar into the Dutch oven and bring to a boil on medium-high flame.
3. Add squash mixture and stir well. Then, lower the heat and simmer for 5 minutes.
4. Place hot mixture into the hot and sterilized jars.
5. Remove any air bubbles. Wipe rims.
6. Place lids on the jars. Add water into the water bath canner and bring to a boil. Place jars into the water bath canner and bring to a boil. Add more boiled water if required.
7. Cover the water bath canner and process for 15 minutes. Remove the jars from the water bath canner. Let cool it. Make sure that the seal is tight.

Nutrition:

Calories: 40

Carbohydrates: 10g

Protein: 0g

Fats: 0g

174. Thousand Island Relish

Preparation time: 60 minutes   **Cooking time:** 50 minutes   **Servings:** 6 pints jar

Ingredients:

- 6 lbs. cucumbers
- 3 cups white sugar
- 2 lbs. onions
- 1 ½ tsp. celery seeds
- 1 cup finely diced green bell pepper
- 1 ½ tsp. ground turmeric
- ½ cup flour
- 3 tbsp. mustard powder
- 4 tbsp. pickling salt
- 1 ½ tsp. mustard seeds
- 1 cup of water
- 1 cup finely diced red bell pepper
- 3 cups white vinegar

Directions:

1. To prepare the cucumbers, wash them first. Then peel, remove their seeds, and finely dice them. Place the cucumbers in a large bowl. Repeat with the bell peppers as well.
2. Next, peel your onion and finely chop it, too. Add it to the same bowl as the cucumbers and pepper.
3. Mix the vegetables with the salt and cover them with water, then set the bowl aside for 1-2 hours before draining them.
4. Mix all your dry ingredients in a large pot, gradually adding in the wet ingredients.
5. Finally, mix in your vegetables and bring the pot to a boil over medium heat. Reduce the heat and leave the mixture to simmer for 30 minutes until it has thickened.
6. Ladle an equal amount of the sauce into your prepared jars. Be aware of the headspace and any air bubbles. Follow the guidelines on sealing your jars properly.
7. Set your water bath canner to a boil and set the jar inside. Make sure that the water completely submerges the jars before letting it boil again. Once it does, place the lid on top and set the 10 minutes processing timer.
8. Carefully remove the hot jars and set aside to cool for 12-24 hours.

Nutrition:

Calories: 40	Protein: 0g
Carbohydrates: 10g	Fats: 0g

175.   Cranberry Relish

Preparation time: 15 minutes   **Cooking time:** 15 minutes   **Servings:** 2 pints jar

Ingredients:

- 2 cups fresh cranberries, chopped
- 6 Medjool dates, pitted and chopped
- ½ shallot, finely diced
- 1 orange, seeded and chopped
- 4 sage leaves, finely chopped
- 2 tablespoons brown sugar
- 1 cup red wine vinegar
- ¼ cup sugar
- 1 tablespoon salt

Directions:

1. Add the cranberries, dates, shallots, sage leaves and orange to a medium bowl and toss well to combine then set aside. Merge the vinegar, sugar and salt in a small saucepan over medium to high heat and bring to a boil. Set the heat to simmer for 10 minutes then remove from heat. Scoop the cranberry relish three quarter way into the storage cans and top with the vinegar mixture, leaving ¼inch head space.
2. Tightly seal the cans and place in a 15 minutes water bath the let cool in a dry place.

Nutrition:

Calories: 81	Sugars: 17g
Total Fat: 0.1g	Protein: 0.6g
Carbs: 21.6g	

Chapter 10. Chutneys

176. Orange Rhubarb Chutney

Preparation time: 15 minutes **Cooking time:** 1 hour 15 minutes **Servings:** 6 pints jar

Ingredients:
- 10 whole black peppercorns
- 1 tbsp. mustard seeds
- 1 tbsp. pickling spice
- 4 tbsp. orange zest, grated
- ⅔ cup orange juice
- 6 cups rhubarb, chopped
- 5 cups brown sugar
- 3 ½ cups cider vinegar
- 3 cups onion, chopped
- 1 ½ cups raisins
- 2 tbsp. garlic, chopped
- 2 tbsp. ginger root, chopped
- 1 tbsp. curry powder
- 1 tsp. ground allspice

Directions:
1. Add pickling spice, mustard seeds, and peppercorn into the cheesecloth and tie it to create a spice bag. Keep it aside.
2. Mix the ginger, garlic, raisins, onion, vinegar, brown sugar, rhubarb, orange zest, and juice into the saucepan and set to a boil on medium-high flame. Stir well. Lower the heat and boil for 45 minutes.
3. Then, add allspice, reserve spice bag, and curry powder and stir well. Boil for 30 minutes.
4. Add water into the water bath canner and place jars in the boiled water. But do not boil it. Place lids over it.
5. Place hot chutney into the hot jars and remove any air bubble. Wipe the rim of each jar. Place jar in the canner. Process it for 10 minutes.
6. Set off the flame and remove the lid. Let cool for 5 minutes.
7. Remove jars and cool it at room temperature.

Nutrition:
Calories: 40
Carbohydrates: 10g
Protein: 0g
Fats: 0g

177. Rhubarb Chutney

Preparation time: 15 minutes **Cooking time:** 15 minutes **Servings:** 6 pints jar

Ingredients:
- 8 cups sliced rhubarb
- 6 cups sliced onion
- 2 cups raisins
- 7 cups light brown sugar
- 4 cups apple cider vinegar
- 2 tbsps. salt
- 2 tsps. cinnamon
- 2 tsps. ginger
- 1 tsp. ground cloves
- ⅛ tsp. cayenne pepper

Directions:
1. Mix all the components together in a large pot.
2. Boil, then simmer gently until the liquid is slightly thickened.
3. Pour into sterile jars and wipe the rims.
4. Tighten the lids and process in a hot water bath for 10 minutes.

Nutrition:
Calories: 58
Fat: 1g
Carbs: 12g
Protein: 0g

178.   Mango Chutney

Preparation time: 15 minutes   **Cooking time:** 45 minutes   **Servings:** 4 pints jar

Ingredients:

- 6 cups sliced green mangos
- ½ lb. fresh ginger
- 3 ½ cups currants
- 8 cups sugar
- 2 cups vinegar
- 3 cups ground cayenne pepper
- 1 cup salt

Directions:

1. Peel the ginger and halve it.
2. Slice one half of the ginger into thin slices; chop the other half of the ginger roughly.
3. Grind the sliced ginger with half of the currants using a blender until well combined. Place all in a saucepan, except the mangoes.
4. Cook over medium heat for 15 minutes.
5. Meanwhile, to set 6 cups, cut, halve, pit, and slice the green mangos.
6. After 15 minutes of cooking, attach the mangos and parboil for another 30 minutes until the mangos are tender.
7. Pour into shot glasses, clean the rims, and screw the lids and rings together.
8. Use the boiling water bath process: pints and quarts for 10 minutes in both.

Nutrition:

Calories: 37   Carbs: 12g

Fat: 0g   Protein: 0g

179.   Apple and Fig Chutney

Preparation time: 10 minutes   **Cooking time:** 2 hours 10 minutes   **Servings:** 4 pints jar

Ingredients:

- 2 lbs. honey crisp apples
- ¼ tsp. cayenne pepper
- ½ tsp. ground cinnamon
- 1 lb. dried figs
- 1 large garlic clove
- 1 tsp. grated fresh ginger
- 2 ½ cups honey
- 1 cup fresh orange juice
- 1 lemon
- 1 tbsp. pomegranate molasses
- 1 tbsp. mustard seed
- ½ tsp. freshly grated nutmeg
- 1 large yellow onion
- 1 cup golden raisins
- 2 cups apple cider vinegar

Directions:

1. Before beginning the canning process, wash your ingredients and prepare your canning equipment.
2. Leave your apples unpeeled, but core and chop them into bite-size pieces. Stem and chop your figs as well. Finely dice your onion and garlic clove. Zest and juice the lemon.
3. Set a pot on medium heat and attach in the honey and vinegar. Mix the liquid until it boils.
4. Stir in the rest of your ingredients and allow it to come back to a boil. Simmer for 2 hours. Stir occasionally.
5. Divide the chutney into your sterilized jars and leave some headspace. Seal and tighten as per the processing Instructions.
6. Fill your water canner halfway with water and let it boil. Carefully insert the jars into the hot water, making sure that they're fully submerged. Wait for the water to boil before closing the canner and starting the 10 minutes processing time.
7. Safely remove the jars and set aside to cool.

Nutrition:

Calories: 85

Carbs: 22.1g

Fat: 0g

Protein: 0.1g

180.   Ginger Apple Chutney

Preparation time: 20 minutes   **Cooking time:** 45 minutes   **Servings:** 3 half-pints jar

Ingredients:

- 2 lbs. apples
- 1½ tsp. freshly grated ginger
- 1 lemon's zest and juice
- 1 tbsp. mustard seed
- 1 cup diced yellow onion

- ¾ cup golden raisins
- ¼ - ½ tsp. crushed red pepper flakes
- ¾ tsp. salt
- 1 cup light brown sugar
- ¾ cup red wine vinegar

Directions:

1. Wash and peel your apples before dicing them into small pieces.
2. Set a large pot on high heat and add all your ingredients. Let the pot come to a boil, cover, and then reduce the heat to low and allow it to simmer for 20 minutes.
3. When the timer has finished, uncover the pot and stir it. Set the heat to medium as you want to keep the mixture at a constant simmer. Cook uncovered for 20-40 minutes until it's thickened.
4. The next step is optional. If you wish to purée the chutney, do so in this step, otherwise move on to the packing stage.
5. Ladle the chutney equally into your jars. Check the headspace before removing any air bubbles and closing them. Tighten your jars correctly.
6. Set your containers in the boiling water of your canner. They should be fully surrounded by water. Set it to come to a boil again, seal the lid, and set a timer for 15 minutes.
7. Remove and cool the jars as per the canning Instructions.

Nutrition:

Calories: 50

Carbs: 0g

Fat: 0g

Protein: 0g

181.   Kiwi Chutney

Preparation time: 60 minutes   **Cooking time:** 10 minutes   **Servings:** 7 pints jar

Ingredients:

- 3 apples, peeled, cored, and chopped
- 1 ½ cups onion, chopped
- 6 cups kiwifruit
- 1 ½ cups cider vinegar
- 1 ½ cups granulated sugar
- ¾ cup dark brown sugar
- ½ cup raisins

- 4 garlic cloves, minced
- 1 tsp. gingerroot, minced
- 1 ½ tsp. cinnamon, ground
- 1 tsp. mustard seed
- ½ tsp. cayenne pepper, cloves, and allspice
- ¼ tsp. pepper and salt

Directions:

1. Peel and chop kiwifruit.
2. Mix the prepared kiwifruit and remaining ingredients into the saucepan, bring to a boil, and stir well for 50 to 60 minutes.
3. Place chutney into the hot and sterilized jars.
4. Remove any air bubbles. Wipe rims.
5. Place lids on the jars. Add water into the water bath canner and bring to a boil. Place jars into the water bath canner and bring to a boil. Add more boiled water if required.
6. Cover the water bath canner and process for 10 minutes. Remove the jars from the water bath canner. Let cool it. Make sure that the seal is tight.

Nutrition:

Calories: 50

Fat: 0g

Carbs: 0g

Protein: 0g

182.   Vinegary Peach Chutney

Preparation time: 25 minutes   **Cooking time:** 60 minutes   **Servings:** 6 pints jar

Ingredients:

- 5 pounds (2.3 kg) yellow peaches, or nectarines, peeled, pitted, and cut into ½ inch dice
- 2 cups sugar
- 1 ½ cups apple cider vinegar
- 1 cup chopped sweet onion
- ¾ cup raisins
- 2 or 3 jalapeño peppers, diced
- 1 sweet banana pepper, or ½ yellow bell pepper, diced
- 3 tablespoons mustard seed
- 2 tablespoons grated fresh ginger
- 2 garlic cloves, minced
- 1 teaspoon garam masala
- ½ teaspoon ground turmeric

Directions:

1. Set a hot water bath. Bring the jars in it to keep warm. Clean the lids and rings in hot, soapy water, and set aside.
2. In a deep pot or a preserving pot set over medium heat, combine the peaches, sugar, cider vinegar, onion, raisins, jalapeños, banana pepper, mustard seed, ginger, garlic, garam masala, and turmeric. Slowly bring to a boil, stirring frequently. Reduce the heat to low. Parboil for 1 hour, or until very thick.
3. Ladle the chutney into the prepared jars, leaving ¼ inch of headspace. Use a nonmetallic utensil to free any air bubbles. Clean the rims and seal with the lids and rings.
4. Set the jars in a hot water bath for 10 minutes. Set off the heat and let the jars rest in the water bath.
5. Carefully detach the jars from the hot water canner. Set aside to cool for 12 hours.
6. Check the lids for proper seals. Detach the rings, wipe the jars, label and date them, and transfer to a cupboard or pantry.
7. For the best flavor, allow the chutney to cure for 3 to 4 weeks before serving. Properly secured jars will last in the cupboard for 12 months. Once opened, refrigerate and consume within 6 weeks.

Nutrition:

Calories: 58

Fat: 1g

Carbs: 12g

Protein: 0g

183.   Jalapeño Pepper Relish

Preparation time: 14 minutes   **Cooking time:** 0 minutes   **Servings:** 8 pints jar

Ingredients:

- 5 pounds (2.3 kg) finely chopped jalapeño peppers
- 2 cups sugar
- 4 cups white vinegar
- ½ cup cilantro leaves (optional)

Directions:

1. In a food processor, finely slice the peppers. Don't turn them into a pureed mush; make them the consistency of a relish.
2. In a large pot, stir the sugar into the vinegar and bring to a boil. Immediately turn off the heat once boil is achieved.
3. Use your food processor to slice the cilantro leaves, if you are using them, then stir them into your chopped peppers.
4. Ladle the uncooked peppers and cilantro into your canning jars, then spoon the liquid over the mixture, allowing ½ inch of headspace.

5. Set the jars in a water bath canner for 10 minutes, adjusting for altitude.

Nutrition:

Calories: 36.1   Protein: 0g

Total fat: 0g   Sugars: 9g

Carbs: 10g   Fiber: 0g

---

184.   Cucumber Relish with Pepper

Preparation time: 14 minutes   **Cooking time:** 13 minutes   **Servings:** 6 pints jar

Ingredients:

- 4 pounds (1.8 kg) finely chopped pickling cucumbers
- ½ cup canning salt
- ½ cup white vinegar
- 2 ⅓ cups sugar

- 4 tablespoons mustard seeds
- 3 cloves garlic, finely minced
- 2 tablespoons celery seeds
- 2 cups diced red bell pepper
- 2 cups finely chopped white onion

Directions:

1. Place cucumbers in a large glass bowl and stir in the salt. Allow them to sit on the counter at room temperature for 4 hours.
2. Drain cucumbers and rinse in a colander under cold water, squeezing out the excess water with your hands.
3. Combine garlic, sugar, mustard seeds, celery seeds, and white vinegar in a saucepan and bring to a boil.
4. Reduce heat and stir in cucumbers, onions, and peppers, then return to a full boil.
5. Reduce heat and simmer the mixture for 10 minutes.
6. Ladle the hot relish into pint or half pints jar, allowing ½ inch of headspace.
7. Secure the jars and process in a hot water bath canner for 10 minutes, adjusting for altitude.

Nutrition:

Calories: 88   Fat: 0g

Protein: 0g   Carbs: 23g

Fiber: 0g

---

185.   Tamarind Chutney

Preparation time: 60 minutes   **Cooking time:** 15 minutes   **Servings:** 3 pints jar

Ingredients:

- 2 tbsp. cumin seeds
- 1 ¼ lbs. dried tamarind
- 3 cups granulated sugar
- 1 cup sultana raisins, rinsed

- 4 tsp. ginger, grated
- 2 ½ tsp. salt
- ¼ tsp. ground black pepper
- 1 tsp. cayenne powder

Directions:

1. Break dried tamarind into chunks into the bowl. Let soak for 20 minutes. Break up tamarind under water with your fingers.
2. Spill it through a strainer into the bowl. Measure three cups of tamarind pulp.
3. Add cumin seeds into the frying pan and cook on high flame, about 2 minutes. Transfer it to the bowl. Let cool it. Add coffee or spice mill and grind it.
4. Add cayenne pepper, black pepper, salt, ginger, raisins, sugar, roasted cumin, and tamarind pulp into the saucepan and bring to a boil. Remove from the flame.
5. Place hot mixture into the hot and sterilized jars.
6. Remove any air bubbles. Wipe rims.

7. Place lids on the jars. Add water into the water bath canner and bring to a boil. Place jars into the water bath canner and bring to a boil. Add more boiled water if required.
8. Cover the water bath canner and process for 15 minutes. Remove the jars from the water bath canner. Let cool it. Make sure that the seal is tight.

Nutrition:

Calories: 170

Fat: 3g

Carbs: 23g

Protein: 14g

186.   Plum Chutney

Preparation time: 15 minutes   **Cooking time:** 50 minutes   **Servings:** 8 half pints

Ingredients:

- 4 cups plums, chopped
- 1 cup onion, minced
- 2 teaspoons fresh ginger, grated
- ¾ cup raisins
- 2 cups brown sugar
- 1½ cups apple cider vinegar

- 2 teaspoons lemon zest, grated
- 2 teaspoons sea salt
- 1 teaspoon ground cinnamon
- ½ teaspoon ground cloves
- ½ teaspoon mustard seeds
- ¼ teaspoon red chili flakes

Directions:

1. In a nonreactive saucepan, add all ingredients over high heat and cook until boiling, stirring continuously.
2. Now adjust the heat to medium and cook, covered for about 40–45 minutes, stirring often.
3. In 3 (½-pint) hot sterilized jars, divide the chutney, leaving about ½-inch space from the top.
4. Slide a small knife around the insides of each jar to remove air bubbles.
5. Close each jar with a lid and screw on the ring.
6. Arrange the jars in a boiling water canner and process for about 15 minutes.
7. Remove the jars from water canner and place onto a wood surface several inches apart to cool completely.
8. After cooling with your finger, press the top of each jar's lid to ensure that the seal is tight.
9. The canned chutney can be stored in the refrigerator for up to 1 month.

Nutrition:

Calories: 71

Sugar: 15.9g

Carbs: 17.6g

Protein: 0.3g

Fiber: 0.5g

187.   Garlicky Lime Chutney

Preparation time: 10 minutes   **Cooking time:** 60 minutes   **Servings:** 3 pints jar

Ingredients:

- 12 limes, scrubbed and cut into ½ inch dice
- 12 garlic cloves, thinly sliced lengthwise
- 1 (4 inch) piece fresh ginger, peeled and thinly sliced

- 8 green chili peppers (jalapeños or Serrano's), stemmed, seeded, and thinly sliced
- 1 tablespoon chili powder
- 1 cup distilled white vinegar
- ¾ cup sugar

Directions:

1. Prepare a hot water bath. Bring the jars in it to keep warm. Clean the lids and rings in hot, soapy water, and set aside.
2. In a medium saucepan, combine the limes, garlic, ginger, chiles, and chili powder, stir well, and bring to a simmer.

3. Add the vinegar and sugar, return to a simmer, and cook, stirring occasionally, until the limes are tender and the mixture is thick to mound when dropped from a spoon, about 70 minutes. Remove from the heat.
4. Ladle the chutney into the prepared jars, leaving ¼ inch of headspace. Use a nonmetallic utensil to free any air bubbles. Clean the rims and seal with the lids and rings.
5. Set the jars in a hot water bath for 20 minutes. Set off the heat and let the jars rest in the water bath.
6. Carefully detach the jars from the hot water canner. Set aside to cool for 12 hours.
7. Check the lids for proper seals. Remove the rings, wipe the jars, label and date them, and transfer to a cupboard or pantry.
8. For the best flavor, allow the chutney to rest for 3 days before serving. Set in refrigerator any jars that don't seal properly and use within 6 weeks. Properly secure jars will last in the cupboard for 12 months. Once opened, refrigerate and consume within 6 weeks.

Nutrition:

Calories: 58

Carbs: 12g

Fat: 1g

Protein: 0g

---

188.   Pungent Tomato Pear Chutney

Preparation time: 45 minutes   **Cooking time:** 10 minutes   **Servings:** 5 pints jar

Ingredients:

- 2 lbs. pears, peeled, chopped
- 2 lbs. tomatoes, peeled, seeded, chopped
- 1 cup finely chopped seeded jalapeno peppers
- 2 cups chopped onions

- 4 tsp. minced fresh ginger root
- 1-2 tsp. crushed red pepper flakes
- 1 tsp. ground mustard
- 1 cup cider vinegar
- 1 cup brown sugar

Directions:

1. In a Dutch oven, combine all ingredients. Bring to a boil.
2. Reduce heat and simmer for 45-60 minutes, uncovered, until thickened, stirring occasionally.
3. Carefully scoop hot mixture into hot sterilized half pints jar, leaving ½ inch headspace. Remove air bubbles and if necessary, adjust headspace by adding hot mixture. Wipe the rims carefully. Place tops on jars and screw on bands until fingertip tight.
4. Place jars into canner with boiling water, ensuring that they are completely covered with water. Let boil for 10 minutes. Remove jars and cool.

Nutrition:

Carbohydrates: 22g

Sodium: 8mg

Fat: 0g

Calories: 88

Protein: 1g

---

189.   Cilantro Chutney Recipe

Preparation time: 45 minutes   **Cooking time:** 10 minutes   **Servings:** 5 pints jar

Ingredients:

- ½ cup of yogurt (this can be omitted or replaced with a vegan-based version of yogurt)
- Lemon juice, three tablespoons
- Cilantro with stems removed (small branches can be left intact), one bunch

- Mint leaves, about one cup packed
- Ginger, sliced (2 teaspoons)
- Sea salt, ½ teaspoon
- One garlic clove
- One medium-sized jalapeno, sliced finely
- Sugar, ½ teaspoon

Directions:

1. Merge all the ingredients above in a blender with one tablespoon of water.

2. Taste and add more spice as needed, then pour it into a sterilized jar and store in the refrigerator. If you want to substitute the yogurt for a non-dairy alternative, you can add coconut or soy-based yogurt. Tofu is another option to consider.
3. If you wish to preserve for a longer time frame, omit the yogurt entirely and store the chutney in a jar for up to one month in your refrigerator.

Nutrition:

Calories: 88

Fat: 0g

Carbs: 22g

Protein: 1g

190. Indian Apple Chutney

Preparation time: 14 minutes   **Cooking time:** 20 minutes   **Servings:** 6 pints jar

Ingredients:

- 2 pounds of apples (medium in size)
- 1 cup of diced onions (finely diced)
- Allspice, two teaspoons
- Ginger, ground or fresh, about two tablespoons
- Raisins, about 7 cups or two pounds
- Red bell pepper, chopped finely, about one cup
- Mustard seeds, about three tablespoons
- Curry powder, about two teaspoons
- Pickling salt, two teaspoons
- 1 clove of garlic, crushed
- 2 hot peppers, seeds removed and diced finely
- 4 cups of malt vinegar
- Brown sugar, about 4 cups (or less, if you prefer less sugar)

Directions:

1. To prepare, wash, and scrub the apples, then peel, core, and slice. Place the apples in a large cooking pot and cover with water. Wash and slice the onions, removing all the skin, and add to the cooking pot.
2. Repeat the same process with the peppers and add them into the pot with the onions and apples. Pour the remaining ingredients into the cooking pot, including the malt vinegar, and bring the contents to a boil. Once this point is reached, cook for about 2 minutes, then reduce to a simmer and stir often.
3. Continue this process until the apples are tender, which can take up to one hour. Place the mixture into sterilized jars and adjust to allow for one inch of space at the top. Clean down the rims of the jars before scooping the contents of the chutney into the jars. Place the lids on tightly and process in a water bath canner for 10-11 minutes. Allow the jars to cool on a wire rack or cloth overnight, then store in a pantry or fruit cellar for up to one month.

Nutrition:

Calories: 47

Carbs: 11.1g

Fat: 0g

Protein: 0g

191. Plum Tomato Chutney

Preparation time: 15 minutes   **Cooking time:** 15 minutes   **Servings:** 4 pints jar

Ingredients:

- 4 tomatoes, chopped
- 6 plums, seeded and chopped
- 2 green chilies, chopped
- 4 tablespoons fresh ginger, grated
- 1 teaspoon lemon zest
- Juice of 1 lemon
- 2 bay leaves
- Pinch of salt
- ½ cup plus 2 tbsp. brown sugar
- 2 teaspoons vinegar
- Pinch black pepper
- 4 tsps. vegetable oil

Directions:

1. Heat the oil in a deep saucepan. Add the bay leaves, ginger and green chilies, and stir. Add the tomatoes, plums. Add the salt, zest, lemon juice and vinegar. Stir in the sugar and pepper, cover, and cook for 3 minutes.
2. Spoon the chutney into sterilized jars, leaving a ½ inch headspace. Wipe the edge of the jar rim clean and add the lid. Process these in a boiling water bath for 10 minutes.

Nutrition:

Calories: 70

Fat: 0g

Carbs: 31g

Protein: 1g

192.   Curried Apple Chutney

Preparation time: 15 minutes   **Cooking time:** 15 minutes   **Servings:** 6 pints jar

Ingredients:

- 2 quarts apples, peeled, cored and chopped
- 2 pounds raisins
- 4 cups brown sugar
- 1 cup onion, chopped
- 1 cup sweet pepper, chopped
- 3 tbsps. mustard seed

- 2 tbsps. ground ginger
- 2 tsps. allspice
- 2 tsps. curry powder
- 2 tsps. salt
- 2 hot red peppers, chopped
- 1 clove garlic, minced
- 4 cups vinegar

Directions:

1. In a large saucepan, mix all the ingredients together. Set to a boil and simmer for 1 hour.
2. Spoon the chutney into sterilized jars, leaving a ½ inch headspace. Wipe the jars' edge rim clean and add the lid. Set jars in a water bath for 10 minutes.

Nutrition:

Calories: 23

Fat: 0g

Carbs: 11g

Protein: 0g

193.   Fruit Chutney

Preparation time: 15 minutes   **Cooking time:** 15 minutes   **Servings:** 6 pints jar

Ingredients:

- 1 tbsp. canola oil
- 4 cups onion, chopped
- 1 tbsp. garlic, minced
- 8 cups prepared fresh fruits, peeled including pears, peaches, tomatoes and apples

- 1 cup mixed dried fruits, chopped
- 1 cup granulated sugar
- 1 cup white vinegar
- 1 cup water
- 1 tsp. crushed red pepper
- 1 tsp. salt

Directions:

1. In a large pan, warmth the oil and cook the onion about 6 minutes. Attach the garlic and stir for 30 seconds. Stir in the fresh fruit, dried fruit, sugar, vinegar, water, red pepper flakes, and salt. Set this to a boil, stirring often, then reduce heat and simmer for 30 minutes.
2. Spoon the chutney into sterilized jars to within ½ inch of the rim. Clean the rims and set the lids on each jar. Process the jars in a water bath for 15 minutes.

Nutrition:

Calories: 47

Fat: 0g

Carbs: 11.1g

Protein: 0g

194.   Green Tomato Chutney

Preparation time: 15 minutes   **Cooking time:** 15 minutes   **Servings:** 3 pints jar

Ingredients:

- 2-½ pounds firm green tomatoes, chopped
- 1-¼ cups brown sugar, packed
- 1 cup red onion, chopped
- 1 cup golden raisins
- 1 cup cider vinegar
- 2 tbsps. candied ginger, minced
- 1 tbsp. mustard seeds
- 1 tsp. chili pepper flakes
- 1 tsp. fennel seeds
- 1 tsp. salt
- ½ tsp. ground allspice
- ⅛ tsp. ground cloves
- 1 cinnamon stick
- Pinch of ground nutmeg

Directions:

1. Set all the ingredients in a 4-quart pot. Bring to a boil and then reduce to a simmer. Secure the pot and cook for 45 minutes.
2. Spoon the chutney into sterilized jars, filling them to ¼ inch from the rim. Wipe the rims clean and set lids on the jars. Process for 15 minutes in a boiling water bath.

Nutrition:

Calories: 18.2   Carbs: 6g

Fat: 0g   Protein: 0g

195.   Cantaloupe Chutney

Preparation time: 15 minutes   **Cooking time:** 90 minutes   **Servings:** 5 pints jar

Ingredients:

- 3 Medium cantaloupes
- 1 pound of dried apricots
- 1 fresh hot chili
- 2 cups of raisins
- 1 tsp. ground cloves
- 1 tsp. ground nutmeg
- 2 tbsps. salt
- 2 tbsps. mustard seed
- ¼ cup fresh ginger, chopped
- 3 cloves garlic
- 4 ½ cups apple cider vinegar
- 2 ¼ cups brown sugar
- 4 onions
- ½ cup orange juice
- 2 tbsps. orange zest

Directions:

1. Thinly cut the apricots and put them into a large bowl.
2. Slice the ginger and garlic thinly and add to the dish.
3. Stir in chili, seed, and dice, and attach to the pot.
4. Attach raisins, cloves, cinnamon, nutmeg, and mustard seeds.
5. Mix and set aside.
6. Merge the vinegar and sugar in a non-reactive pot or kettle; bring to boil over medium heat.
7. Attach mixture to the pot in a bowl and return to a moderate simmer.
8. Keep simmer for 45 minutes. Do not deck the pot.
9. Meanwhile, onions are sliced and placed in a bowl.
10. Cantaloupes fifth, peel, and seed.
11. Set the fruit into cubes of ½ Add onions.
12. In cup, attach orange juice and zest; mix well.
13. Once the vinegar mixture has ended 45 minutes of cooking time, add the cantaloupe mixture to the bowl, bring it back to a cooler, and start cooking for another 45 minutes or until thickened at the simmer.
14. Pour into hot glasses, clean the rims, screw the lids and rings together.
15. Boiling water bath process: pints and quarts 10 minutes in both.

Nutrition:

Calories: 54   Fat: 0g

Carbs: 14g   Protein: 1g

196.   Spicy Green Tomato Chutney

Preparation time: 15 minutes   **Cooking time:** 15 minutes   **Servings:** 3 pints jar

Ingredients:

- 2 ½ cups spiced cider vinegar
- 3 cups shallots, finely chopped
- 2 quarters small green tomatoes, peeled and thinly sliced
- 1 tsp. celery salt
- 4 cups finely chopped apples

- 2 sweet red or green peppers
- Dry, hot chilies (four to six depending on heat strength)
- 2 ¼ cups brown sugar
- 2 cups ripe tomatoes, peeled and chopped
- salt

Directions:

1. Combine 2 ½ cups of apple cider vinegar, 1 stick of cinnamon, 1 teaspoon of allspice, whole cloves, black peppercorns, and ½ teaspoon ground nutmeg in a medium ability boiling pot.
2. Set the fire on, and nearly get it to the boil.
3. Detach from the heat immediately and allow to cool down to room temperature.
4. Strain before applying to the chutney.
5. Black tomatoes to be peeled:
6. Place bowl, pot, or kettle in heat-proof.
7. Pour over boiling water to cover, letting them rest for three minutes.
8. Pierce peel with a sharp knife's tip and pull off the skin.
9. Slice very thinly on those tomatoes.
10. Pour in a colander over a tub, or green tomato slices with salt in a sink plate.
11. Let them drain for two hours.

In the meantime:

1. Skin chop the apples sweet, core, and finely to make 4 cups.
2. A place to ready for use in acidulated water.
3. Clean shallots, then finely chop them to make 3 cups.
4. Prepare sweet peppers by washing, seeding, halving, and de rib.
5. Place under broiler or over open flames until the skin is charred and fleece away. Remove peppers; slice them thinly.
6. Place the chilies in a bag with cheesecloth.
7. Rinse green tomatoes at the end of two hours.
8. Combine green tomato slices, spiced strained vinegar, shallots, apples, hot chili bag, brown sugar, and celery salt in a large bowl.
9. Set to a boil, cook for 15 minutes or until most of the liquid has evaporated.
10. Remove broiled, ripe tomatoes, and sweet peppers.
11. Simmer for about an hour, until dark.
12. Remove the bag of chili.
13. Pour into shot glasses, clean the rims, screw the lids and rings together.
14. Boiling water bath process: pints and quarts 10 minutes in both.

Nutrition:

Calories: 236   Carbs: 22g

Fat: 0g   Protein: 0.6g

197.   Black Currant

Preparation time: 15 minutes   **Cooking time:** 30 minutes   **Servings:** 3 pints jar

Ingredients:

- 4 ½ cups black currants, crushed
- ¼ cup lemon juice

- 3 cups granulated sugar
- 1 cup water
- 1 tablespoon lemon zest
- Pinch of salt

Directions:
1. Combine the ingredients in a deep saucepan or cooking pot.
2. Boil the mixture and cook for about 30 minutes over medium heat until firm and thick. Stir continually to prevent scorching.
3. Spill the hot mixture into pre-sterilized jars directly or with a jar funnel. Keep headspace of ¼ inch from the jar top.
4. To detach tiny air bubbles, insert a nonmetallic spatula and stir the mixture gently.
5. Clean the sealing edges with a cloth. Secure the jars with the lids and adjust the bands/rings to seal and prevent any leakage.
6. Set the jars in a hot water bath for 10 minutes.
7. Set the jars in a cool, dry and dark place. Allow them to cool down completely.
8. Store in your refrigerator.

Nutrition:

Calories: 47

Fat: 0g

Carbs: 11.1g

Protein: 0g

198. Watermelon Lemon

Preparation time: 15 minutes   **Cooking time:** 30 minutes   **Servings:** 3 pints jar

Ingredients:
- 2 pounds watermelon, peeled, seeded and cubed
- 3 cups white sugar
- 3 lemons, unpeeled, sliced and seeded

Directions:
1. In a deep saucepan or cooking pot, merge the watermelon cubes, lemons and sugar.
2. Boil the mixture; cook for about 2 hours over medium heat until firm and thick. Stir continually to prevent scorching.
3. Spill the hot mixture into pre-sterilized jars directly or with a jar funnel. Keep headspace of ¼ inch from the jar top.
4. To detach tiny air bubbles, insert a nonmetallic spatula and stir the mixture gently.
5. Clean the sealing edges with a damp cloth. Secure the jars with the lids and adjust the bands/rings to seal and prevent any leakage.
6. Set the jars in a hot water bath for 10 minutes.
7. Set the jars in a cool, dry and dark place. Allow them to cool down completely.
8. Store in your refrigerator.

Nutrition:

Calories: 36.1

Total fat: 0g

Carbs: 10g

Protein: 0g

Sugars: 9g

Fiber: 0g

199. Tangy Tomato

Preparation time: 15 minutes   **Cooking time:** 30 minutes   **Servings:** 3-4 pints jar

Ingredients:
- 1 cup sugar
- ¾ cup honey
- 2 medium lemons, unpeeled, chopped and seeded
- 2 ½ pounds yellow tomatoes
- 2 ounces ginger, grated

Directions:
1. In a deep saucepan or cooking pot, merge the water and tomatoes.

2. Boil the mixture; simmer over low heat to soften the tomatoes.
3. Peel the skin, remove the seeds, and finely chop the tomatoes.
4. In a deep saucepan or cooking pot, merge the chopped tomatoes, honey and sugar.
5. Set aside for a few hours.
6. Add the lemons and ginger.
7. Boil the mixture; cook over medium heat until firm and thick. Swirl continually to prevent scorching.
8. Spill the hot mixture into pre-sterilized jars directly or with a jar funnel. Keep headspace of ¼ inch from the jar top.
9. To free tiny air bubbles, set a nonmetallic spatula and swirl the mixture.
10. Clean the sealing edges with a damp cloth. Secure the jars with the lids and adjust the bands/rings to seal and prevent any leakage.
11. Set the jars in a hot water bath for 5 minutes.
12. Bring the jars in a cool, dry and dark place. Allow them to cool down completely.
13. Store in your refrigerator.

Nutrition:

Calories: 36.1

Total fat: 0g

Carbs: 10g

Protein: 0g

Sugars: 9g

Fiber: 0g

Sodium: 227.1mg

Potassium: 0mg

200.   Tangy Mango Chutney

Preparation time: 10 minutes   **Cooking time:** 20 minutes   **Servings:** 4-6 pints jar

Ingredients:

- ½ cup diced red bell pepper
- 1 tbsp. freshly grated ginger
- 6 cups diced mangoes
- ½ cup diced onion
- ¼ tsp. red pepper flakes
- ¾ cup golden raisins
- ½ tsp. salt
- 2 cups granulated sugar
- ½ cup apple cider vinegar

Directions:

1. In a saucepan, merge all your ingredients together and bring them to a boil over medium-high heat. When the mixture is boiling, set the heat to medium and leave it to cook for 20 minutes. The mixture should thicken. Remember to stir occasionally.
2. To check if the consistency is correct, perform the freezer test: place a plate in the freezer, then put a small amount of chutney on it. Place it back into the freezer for 2 minutes and run a spoon through it. If it stays separated, then the chutney is done. If the amount doesn't separate when you run a spoon through it, place the chutney back onto the heat for a few more minutes and perform the test again.
3. Ladle equal amounts of the chutney into your clean jars. Check the headspace before sealing and tightening your jars.
4. Set half a pot of water to a boil in your canner. Slowly place the jars inside and check the level of the water. The jars should be completely covered. Allow the water to boil again, close the lid, and start a timer for 10 minutes.

Nutrition:

Calories: 170

Carbs: 23g

Fat: 3g

Protein: 14g

Chapter 11.   Measurement

1. Food Reference Chart

Type of Food	Pint Processing Time	Quart Processing Time	*Headspace*
Asparagus	30 minutes	40 minutes	1 inch
Beans, Lima	40 minutes	50 minutes	1-1.5 inches
Beans, Green	20 minutes	25 minutes	1 inch
Beets	30 minutes	35 minutes	1 inch
Carrots	25 minutes	30 minutes	1 inch
Corn kernels	55 minutes	85 minutes	1 inch
Peas	40 minutes	50 minutes	1 inch
Peppers	35 minutes	40 minutes	1 inch
Potatoes	35 minutes	40 minutes	1 inch
Pumpkin	55 minutes	90 minutes	1 inch
Spinach and other greens	70 minutes	90 minutes	1 inch
Vegetable soups	60 minutes	75 minutes	1 inch
Ground meat	75 minutes	90 minutes	1 inch
Meat Strips, cubes or	75 minutes	90 minutes	1 inch
Poultry without bones	75 minutes	90 minutes	1 ¼ inch
Poultry with bones	65 minutes	75 minutes	1 ¼ inch
Meat soups	75 minutes	90 minutes	1 inch
Meat stock	20 minutes	25 minutes	1 inch
Fish	100 minutes	110 minutes	1 inch
Okra	25 minutes	40 minutes	1 inch

2. Fruit Chart

*Note: Headspace for all fruit cooked in a pressure canner is ½ inch.

Fruit	Pint and Quart Minutes
Apples	8 minutes
Applesauce	5 minutes
Berries	8 minutes
Cherries	8 minutes
Cranberries	8 minutes
Figs	10 minutes
Grapes	8 Minutes
Peaches	8 minutes
Pears	8 minutes
Persimmons	10 minutes
Pineapple	8 minutes
Plums	8 minutes
Prunes	8 minutes
Quinces	12 minutes
Raspberries	8 minutes
Rhubarb	5 minutes
Strawberries	5 minutes
Tomatoes	10 minutes
Fruit juices	5 minutes

Index Recipes

BONUS: VIDEO LECTURES

Water Bath canning is an amazing way to preserve food. So, we thought that you would appreciate having some video lectures to consult to furtherly clarify some of the concepts discussed in this book.

You can find them at this link:

Video Lecture Link

Conclusion

Water bath canning nowadays is used primarily for home canning to preserve food's flavor and nutritional value. It is a very safe way to preserve food because it does not use any chemicals. The only things that are in the jars are the acid and other preservatives if you choose. This method produces good results in preserving food from bacteria because the jars are boiled whole, killing all harmful germs and microorganisms that cause spoiling or decay. The steps use steam under pressure to cook food that is placed into a sealed jar. The jars are then placed into boiling water for a specified time to sterilize and seal the jars.

Water bath canning is a technique that requires you to use water to sterilize jars and covers during the sealing process. This method of properly preserving foods uses high heat and pressure as two-part barriers for keeping bacteria out of food, typically done in a boiling water bath canner. Food preserved using this technique retains its natural color, flavor, nutritional value, texture, and other properties. Water bath canning is one of the safest ways of preserving food. Canning is a method of food preservation that uses heat to destroy microorganisms that cause food spoilage and the growth of harmful bacteria. While this is done through heat, it does not cook or pasteurize the food. Instead, it creates an acidic environment that inhibits the growth of food-spoiling microorganisms.

The jars must be boiled and then placed into a water bath to be sterilized. Before canning, you should make sure that your jars are clean, free from rust or other debris, and screw on tight. Store them upside down, so the mouth is at the bottom of the jar. Place lids on the jars and place them in a boiling water canner for about 30 minutes.

Thank you for using this book to learn about water bath canning. Make sure to always follow proper steps and safety procedures while canning food. Make sure that you have the felicitous equipment and do not ignore any steps in this process. As long as you come after the instructions carefully and safely, you'll be sure to enjoy food that has been preserved adequately for months to come.

If you enjoyed this book, we would really appreciate a review:
Review Link

Manufactured by Amazon.ca
Bolton, ON